Conventional Teaching and Assessment Guide

Sue Bodman and Glen Franklin

University Printing House, Cambridge CB2 8BS, United Kingdom

One Liberty Plaza, 20th Floor, New York, NY 10006, USA

477 Williamstown Road, Port Melbourne, VIC 3207, Australia

314–321, 3rd Floor, Plot 3, Splendor Forum, Jasola District Centre, New Delhi – 110025, India

79 Anson Road, #06–04/06, Singapore 079906

Cambridge University Press is part of the University of Cambridge.

It furthers the University's mission by disseminating knowledge in the pursuit of
education, learning and research at the highest international levels of excellence.

Information on this title: www.cambridge.org/9781108647878

© Cambridge University Press and UCL Institute of Education 2019

Learning objectives from the Cambridge Assessment International Education
Primary English curriculum framework are reproduced with the permission of
Cambridge Assessment International Education

First published 2019

20 19 18 17 16 15 14 13 12 11 10 9 8 7 6 5 4 3 2 1

Printed in Great Britain by CPI Group (UK) Ltd, Croydon CR0 4YY

A catalogue record for this publication is available from the British Library

ISBN 978-1-108-64787-8 Conventional Teaching and Assessment Guide with Cambridge Elevate

....

....

Contents

Introduction

Introducing *Cambridge Reading Adventures*

Cambridge Reading Adventures is one of the first Primary reading schemes designed for use by children from all international contexts. To achieve this aim, it moves away from the western-centric approach adopted by many English medium reading schemes. To ensure high quality texts and engaging stories, we went to the very best authors and illustrators from around the world. They have provided an outstanding range and variety of stories and non-fiction. Cambridge Reading Adventures covers the entire Primary age range. This Teaching and Assessment Guide supports the use of four strands for readers aged seven to twelve. The progression is built around curriculum expectations. This pedagogy has been created by Series Editors Sue Bodman and Glen Franklin of the UCL Institute of Education, ensuring that every page of every book is designed to support the reading process and the ultimate goals of reading comprehension and making meaning. The series is accompanied by thorough guidance to the teacher, so that teaching interactions can be planned to develop reading and thinking skills. Cambridge Reading Adventures provides the learner with a range of stories, all of which have the kinds of settings, plots and characters which a child growing anywhere in the world can relate to.

Some stories in the scheme have a contemporary setting, designed to reflect life around the world in the 21st Century that the children will recognise, at school, for example. In the Conventional Stage, there are many stories with less familiar settings including stories about life in a refugee camp or the escape from a volcanic eruption. Whatever the setting, the reader will recognise the relevance to the world of a growing child; friendship and disagreement, success and disappointment and the challenges of inclusion.

Other stories draw on the rich seams of traditional stories from all around the world. The legendary Arabic sailor Sinbad appears in one of the stories, continuing his adventures from the tales in the Transitional readers collection. There are also traditional tales from China, Africa and other parts of the world. Historical settings, such as in 'Hunters of the Sea' provide opportunities to learn about and discuss complex issues, requiring maturity of understanding.

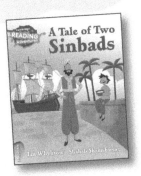
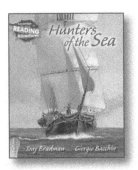

An equally high-quality range of non-fiction titles provides balance and breadth to the series. Titles include a variety of information genre — reports, recounts and persuasive texts — and cover a range of topics of great relevance to the wider curriculum, with full links provided to international curricula in the back of each book. Texts are designed to give readers the opportunity to learn the key skills for navigating non-fiction books, and properly utilising features like tables, maps, fact boxes, captions, indexes and glossaries. Teachers are provided with quality materials to teach these skills.

Great care has been taken to choose topics which are directly relevant to the young child growing up in the 21st Century, such as 'Skyscrapers' and 'The Changing Climate'. Some books offer a glimpse into the past ('The Cave at the End of the World' and 'Inventing the World') and even considering what the future might hold ('Journey to Callisto' and 'Meltdown'). In addition, there is a rich strand of books about the natural world ('Diving under the Waves' and 'Dolphins in the Wild').

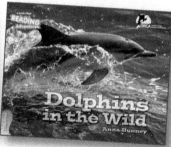

For the teacher, Cambridge Reading Adventures offers a thorough and dependable teaching structure and comprehensive guidance for teaching guided reading. For the developing reader, whether in Bangkok, Dubai, London, Mumbai or Bogota, Cambridge Reading Adventures promises a rich, fully supportive and fascinating journey towards becoming an independent reader.

The UCL Institute of Education's International Literacy Centre (ILC) promotes quality and efficacy in literacy education from age three to thirteen (Early Years Foundation Stage to Key Stage 3). Over the last 25 years, the ILC, formally the European Centre for Reading Recovery, has successfully trained many thousands of teachers, including those from international contexts, to provide effective literacy teaching through a range of interventions and classroom approaches. As well as providing high-quality professional support for teachers and teacher educators, the ILC develops materials and professional development opportunities to support teachers to teach literacy skills effectively. For this scheme, they have developed an innovative progression for older readers in the last four years of primary school. This is organised into strands: Pathfinders, Wayfarers, Explorers and Voyagers. Each of the four strands is designed to meet the needs of an age-related year group in school, providing texts to support the development of skills focused on reading to learn (see pages 16-18 for full guidance). The criteria for creating progression across the four strands involve subject matter, text structure, tone and register and complexity of language and is quite different from the banding progression used for younger readers.

The Cambridge Reading Adventures has three distinct phases of progression; Early, Transitional and Conventional. These combine to offer schools a cohesive progression from the very earliest steps in learning to read to skilled reading and thoughtful responding at around the age of twelve.

Sue Bodman and Glen Franklin, the Series Editors of *Cambridge Reading Adventures*, are National Leaders at the International Literacy Centre

Introduction

Overview of the Teaching and Assessment Guide

The *Cambridge Reading Adventures Teaching and Assessment Guide* is designed to support teachers to deliver effective guided reading lessons, and to make meaningful assessments that serve to ensure children achieve success.

The Teaching and Assessment Guide is divided into three sections:

Section One: Teaching Reading

This section explores the nature of reading. Based on the underlying principle that reading is a meaningful activity carried out for purpose and pleasure, the range of reading in classrooms is explored and the different features of fiction and non-fiction reading are considered. The nature of guided reading as a specific teaching method is explained. The philosophy and practice of providing a progression in strands is outlined, with clear examples provided.

This section is predominantly to inform teachers, and provides the theoretical background to the teaching approach employed in *Cambridge Reading Adventures*.

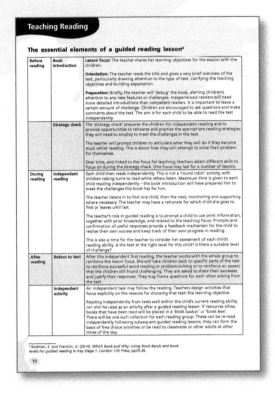

Section Two: Book By Book Overview

Each individual text in *Cambridge Reading Adventures* is explained in detail, helping teachers to select the right book for the right group of children. Teaching guidance is provided for the fiction and non-fiction texts at each strand.

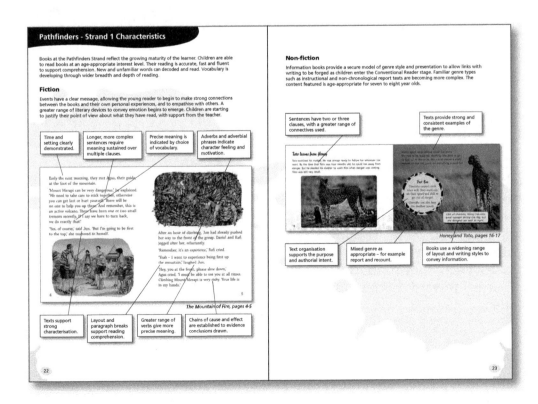

Section Three: Assessment for guided reading

This section offers a selection of comprehension questions, covering a range of question types. These can be used either as a discrete assessment resource, or to support teaching for specific comprehension objectives during guided reading lessons.

A range of support materials is provided to assess the child's proficiency with the particular strand. Exemplars to support implementing this assessment process are also included for fiction and non-fiction.

Pathfinders Strand 1
Comprehension Assessment

Name: Abida
Class Group: Tigers
Date: 07.12.17

Title *River Rescue*

Summarising task:
Abida retold the story confidently and in the correct sequence. She referred to the text to clarify a few details, such as which of the two boys went first across the river. She added personal commentary, stating that she thought the two boys were silly to go on the river when the weather forecast was bad, and that their dad should have looked after them.

Reading task
Pages read 10 to 18

Reading Accuracy
Reading generally accurate. Some inflectional 'ed' endings missed but likely to be linked to her pronunciation of these words in English. Some sounding out along words which are unfamiliar to her ('stranded', 'dangled'). On p.16, she missed out the word 'light' then reread the whole sentence to correct this omission. She asked for my help on the words 'skywards' and 'surface'.

Reading Fluency
Abida attended to the text for clues in how to use expression as she read character voices (for example, when Mr Pattama yelled out on p.16). She noted speech punctuation, using this to change her voice when reading as a character. Some more stilted reading of longer narrative sections, and some confusion when reading more complex sentences, such as on p.18.

Questions to assess understanding

Recalling:
Abida said 'they would not have time to get here and the boys might die in the river'.

Understanding vocabulary:
She used the text to help her, and told me, 'it's when the river goes very fast and comes over the sides'. She did not refer to the landslip which contributed to the speed of the flood.

Inferring:
First answered literally ('it would fall in the river'). When prompted was able to give a more inferential answer ('maybe the rope would be near so one of the boys could grab it').

Responding:
Abida thought Kamon was brave: 'he likes doing brave things, and he had a good idea to save the boys'. She was very concerned that the boys should not have been on the river: 'their dad should have not let them'.

Relating to different contexts
Abida was able to answer as the character: 'I think I would be very pleased that I saved the two little boys, but cross with their dad for letting them take their boats in the river'. I asked 'do you think Kamon will go kayaking again?' 'I think he might be scared next time, and he will like to fly his aeroplane (drone) instead'.

Summary of Reading comprehension skills
Abida was able to summarise the story in a short retelling, adding personal detail and opinion. She read mostly accurately. She appealed when words were unknown, but noticed errors of omission, rereading to self-correct. She read speech passages accurately, although found reading longer more complex passages more difficult.

In the comprehension tasks, Abida was able to recall information directly in the text, although needed some prompting to infer what might have happened in the story if the drone had crashed. Her answers were also influenced by her concern for the small boys and why they were out on the river on their own. She didn't note information in the text to aid her definition of a flash flood, but gave a reasonable description.

Recommendations
Abida initially struggled with books in the Pathfinders strand, and previous assessments suggested she remain at that strand. It is pleasing to see the progress she has made over this term, and she is ready to move on. Attention will be needed to maintain fluency especially on longer, more complex sentences, as this may affect her comprehension. Also, to watch for appeals to the teacher, prompting her 'what can you do to solve that word?' or 'what do you know that can help you?' when she stops at unknown words.

Move to Strand 2?
Yes

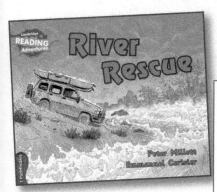

CHAPTER FOUR

Slowly, the drone hovered its way
across the river towards the stranded boys.
The rope dangled just above the swirling currents.

'I hope the drone can make it before
the power runs out,' said Kamon.

The drone reached the rock where
the two boys were stranded.

'Unhook the rope!' Mr Pattama yelled out,
as the drone hovered above them.

The eldest boy stood up and tried to reach
the rope but he couldn't do it.
The battery warning level light began to flash faster.

'Come on, grab it,' Kamon breathed.

16

17

SECTION 1: TEACHING READING

What is Reading?

When you pick up a book, open a web-link or read a set of instructions, what is it that directs what you are doing? You will have had a purpose in mind that shapes how you read and what you do – you might want to settle down and read your new novel, or to check what time your flight is, or you might need to set up your new tablet computer. Sometimes reading will be for pleasure, sometimes for work or to glean information; each of these purposes requires you to read, but in a subtly different way.

In this Teaching and Assessment Guide, we define reading as a process by which the reader gains meaning from the printed word[1]. Reading is a complex act, whatever the purpose and whatever the age of the reader: it requires the control of many aspects – the ability to match letters to their corresponding sound (grapheme/phoneme correspondence); to blend sounds together to make words; to look for known parts in longer, multisyllabic words; to read sentences, understanding how word order, punctuation and vocabulary choice all serve to convey the author's intention; to know how texts are constructed and to understand their purpose and meaning.

This complex task of reading starts with looking[2]. Beginner readers need to learn how print works. They have to attend to those black squiggles on a white page, to know that they track one-to-one accurately across a line of text from left-to-right in English, to begin to notice letters and words they know, and to understand that what they say has to match what they can see on the page. As children learn more about the alphabetic code,

they begin to break the words they can see into separate phonemes, blending them together to read the word. They begin to recognise recurring parts of words such as 'ing' and 'ed' and they link what they already know to the new words they encounter. As more and more words become automatically recognised, reading becomes faster and more fluent. The child starts to sound like a reader. As accuracy and fluency develop, the reader can go beyond the 'words on the page' and draw on the text to infer characters' feelings, thoughts and motives from their actions, justifying inferences with evidence. Reading for information takes place on topics that are well beyond the experience of the reader and involve subject-specific and technical vocabulary. Opportunities to read regularly and receive well-timed feedback and encouragement from the teacher are needed long after word reading accuracy with most letter-to-sound relationships has been achieved. Reading is just as much about language processes as it is about word reading processes.

As readers mature and develop fast and fluent word reading skills, accessing the literal meanings in text become easier. But what about the layers of meaning that exist 'under the surface' of text? Thinking about the component parts of comprehension offers a way to understand the reading process of a reader between the ages of eight and twelve. To begin with, each word itself must be read. This is more complex than decoding by matching graphemes to phonemes and then a plausible pronunciation; the reader has to access the context and the specific usage of that word in that place. In English, words have multiple meanings and sometimes

---

[1] Bodman, S. and Franklin, G. (2014). Which Book and Why: Using Book Bands and book levels for guided reading in Key Stage 1. London: IoE Press

[2] Clay, M. M. (2016). Literacy Lessons Designed for Individuals (Second Edition) Auckland, N.Z.: Heinemann

different pronunciations, the precision of each informed by the surrounding context and grammatical structure. For example, 'wind' is uttered differently depending on the meaning and whether we are talking about weather, or a mechanical toy. Using knowledge of letters and words needs to be fast, fluent and flexible, but there are many more skills to be learned, some of which present particular challenge to the second language learner.

Comprehending and making sense of a text is an integrative process; we have to make links between the sequences of sentences we read, often constructing bridges to link between each sentences. Integrating sentence meaning in this way is an important aspect of inference. For example, in the text the reader has to

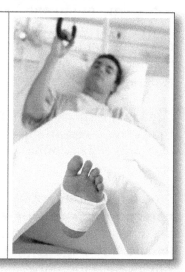

John was at the beach.

He trod on some broken glass.

He had to go to hospital.

understand that 'he' throughout the sentences is John, that the glass was on the beach and the cause of the hospital visit is the injury due to broken glass. None of these things are stated in the text, they are understood by integrating the sentences and resolving the pronoun use.

Comprehension is also a constructive process, in which explicit information in a sentence or group of sentences is supplemented by knowledge about the world from long-term memory. As we read, we construct a mental model, a picture of your general understanding. This means that we don't need to store every word of the text in order to keep reading with the previous meaning in our mind. It also enables us to fill in details of character, setting and potential story structure, through inference.

Comprehension involves metacognitive processes, too. As we read, we might suddenly stop. Something is alerting us to a jarring in what we expected to read and what we have understood. This might be because of our prior knowledge of a topic or a character, or because it doesn't seem to fit with the story structure or language register.

Reading comprehension, therefore, involves the interaction of key processes, all of which are vital in reading with understanding and gaining meaning. Tennent, Reedy, Hobsbaum and Gamble (2016) offer a list of reading components for the teacher to consider as they teach and assess reading comprehension skills:

- Vocabulary
- Grammatical understanding
- Memory
- Inference-making
- Comprehension monitoring
- Background knowledge. (Tennent at al. (2016, page 15)[3]

<hr />

[3] Tennent, Reedy, Hobsbaum and Gamble (2016) Guiding Readers – Layers of Meaning London: IoE Press

Teaching Reading

Whatever the age of the reader, books need to be engaging, motivating and above all pleasurable to read. Classrooms provide many different opportunities for readers to engage in reading for purpose and pleasure throughout the primary school phase. Teachers read and share stories and rhymes. They provide opportunities for children to read and share books with friends, or quietly by themselves. They make available a wealth of reading material, including access to the Internet and the use of information technology. Teachers demonstrate how reading 'works' in shared reading sessions; perhaps showing how to locate information in a book about animals, or looking at how the author made the story more exciting by using some really interesting words. All teaching of reading requires good quality books, whether the teaching context be modelled, shared, guided or independent reading. This Teaching and Assessment Guide focuses specifically on the use of quality texts in guided reading.

Reading Journals

The Cambridge Reading Adventures provide good quality texts for guided reading sessions. They are also designed to offer the context for 'jumping off' into reading, developing a personal reading taste for style and genre. As well as using the range of lesson plans and supporting resources offered in this Teaching and Assessment Guide, Reading Response journals provide opportunities to respond to and interpret their reading on an individual basis. In these journals, teachers encourage readers to generate their own meanings by responding to the texts by composing messages about their own thoughts and reflections. It also provides the context to link Cambridge Reading Adventures books to other texts, both fiction and non-fiction and to gather interesting and thought-provoking words and phrases as a resource for writing. Children can be prompted to ask questions of their own reading, using their background knowledge and experiences to create a personal response and an individual reaction. This is then recorded in a reading response journal, providing a link to the 'active', 'constructive' and 'metacognitive' elements of becoming a lifelong reader described above.

A reading journal could be created using notebooks and pens, or set up as electronic documents on a computer or tablet. The important thing is to make sure that each child can 'make it their own', choosing how to present their thoughts and ideas, sometimes illustrating their ideas and responses.

Opportunities to put thoughts into words support active meaning making and deep comprehension. On page 30 – 33 in this Teaching and Assessment Guide, you can find some suggestions for books reviews and reading logs. These are just a few examples of the many kinds of reading journals you can create with children. Use your imagination – and theirs!

Reading journals: the teacher's role

The teacher's role is to establish the purpose for writing an entry in the reading response journal:

Initial responses to the book	What do you think of the book after reading a few pages? How have your impressions changed? Would you recommend the book to others? Why/Why not? Who else should read this book and why?
Comment on particular characters or events in the book	Is there a character that you love or hate? Are the characters true to life? What has the author done to create that reality?
Link events or facts in the book to the reader	Does this book remind you of another book you've read? Or something that's happened to you?
Use the text as a resource for writing	Does the book have some good phrases and expressions that could be used in writing? How are the sentences structured? What effect do they have on the reader?
Presents differing points of view Draws a conclusion based on the argument presented.	Written in the present tense Connectives link the points being made ('however', 'therefore'). Addresses the reader more generally
Clear statement of the concern to be addressed Logically sequence leading to a conclusion	Written in the present tense Use of powerful, often emotive language to put over the point of view

Reading Fiction Books

Fiction is all about story-telling. As readers, we choose stories that excite, intrigue, puzzle or frighten us. We look for stories that reaffirm our own lives or take us to lives we can only imagine. Haven[4] described stories as 'the primary roadmap for understanding, making sense of, remembering and planning our lives'. What makes a story? It has been said that there are just a small number of basic story themes, and these have been around since humans first began to tell stories: monsters and villains are overcome; the poor become rich through good fortune or wrong-doing; quests are made to seek to do something or to right a wrong; voyages to unknown worlds are undertaken and the adventurer returns to tell the tale. Stories can be funny or tragic, or a mixture of both.

Fiction writers rework or revise these themes to continue to tell new stories. They intermingle the themes – a quest may have elements of comedy; a monster story might have a rags-to-riches ending. Writers take those basic plots and situations and, by reinventing them, they make it their own.

When writing a book, an author always has the potential reader in mind. A book written to be shared by a parent or carer with a young child sitting on her lap will be a very different sort of book to that which an older reader would chose to read on their own in bed at night. The writer's purpose and audience dictate the style, scope, vocabulary and even the length of the text. The fiction books in Cambridge Reading Adventures have been written specifically to be used in a small group guided reading context, led by a teacher, to support the teaching of reading.

Reading is first and foremost about making meaning. In the Early and Transitional stages of Cambridge Reading Adventures, young children are learning to read using short, motivating texts which mirror the natural pattern of spoken language, with words and phrases within the child's conceptual understanding, and which support the development of word reading with strong grammatical structures and clear meaning.

At around the age of 8, the nature of reading changes. Books at the Conventional Stage support this change. Stories have become more complex, using unfamiliar language structures and often include subjects outside of a child's

THE STORY OF SINBAD

For several weeks at sea, Sinbad had bad luck. Sometimes there was no wind and the boat couldn't move at all. Sometimes they ran out of water and the crew fell ill. Sometimes they nearly froze in snow and ice. At last, they sailed into warm blue waters again.

But all of a sudden, a great storm blew up. The ship was blown onto some rocks at the end of a little island.

Luckily, the storm went away just as quickly as it had started, and Sinbad and his crew began to repair their ship. Then they tried to drag it back into the water. Before they could float the ship again, they noticed some people coming towards them.

Sinbad and his crew got ready to fight, but then they saw that the islanders had no weapons. It seemed that they had been hiding in the forest and now they had come down to the beach to welcome the sailors with fresh water and fruit.

12

13

Sinbad

4 Haven, K. (2007: 3). *Story Proof: The Science Behind the Startling Power of Story*. Westport, CT: Libraries Unlimited.

personal experience. Stories have multiple events occurring over time and space, and with fewer illustrations to support the reader's imagination.

Stories require more inferential links to be made. Inference is crucial to reading comprehension. Readers have to move beyond the literal meaning of the actual words on the page, to read 'between the lines' to fully comprehend the author's intention. Kintsch and Rawlson[5] describe this as the reader forming a mental or 'situation' model of the story. Readers, they argue, use their prior knowledge, their understanding of the subject and of how stories work, to fill in the gaps. Fiction books in the Cambridge Reading Adventures have strong story structures to support comprehension. Themes build upon children's own experiences by placing new characters in familiar events, or through traditional retellings of tales from around the world. As books become longer, stories are often sustained over two or more events, or over time. Language structures become more complex, with the meaning sometimes implied by the word order or the author's choice of vocabulary.

Motivation is key to reading comprehension. Wery and Thomson (2013)[6] claim that there is clear evidence linking motivation to strong reading outcomes. Achievement in reading is influenced by the learner's self-efficacy to succeed. Stories in the Conventional Stage of Cambridge Reading Adventures are written to motivate, interest, challenge and excite developing young readers as they continue on their reading journey.

The teaching notes at the back of each book offer guidance to teachers for teaching inference-making in story. Many of the follow-up suggestions provide activities designed to support developing comprehension. This Teaching and Assessment Guide describes each story in detail, and explains the teaching opportunities featured at each strand (see pages 36-108). The supplementary activity sheets provide comprehension and composition work for children to complete independently, either during or after their series of guided reading lessons. 6

Hunters of the Sea

[5] Kintsch, W., & Rawson, K. a. (2005). Comprehension. In M. J. Snowling & C. Hulme (Eds.), The Science of Reading: A Handbook (pp. 209-226). Malden, Ma: Blackwell.

[6] Wery, J., & Thomson, M. (2013). Motivational strategies to enhance effective learning in teaching struggling students. Support For Learning, 28(3), 103 -108.

Reading Non-fiction Books

If we stopped and thought about the reading we have done over the last 24 hours, a large proportion of that reading is likely to have been non-fiction: consulting a recipe book to check the amount of sugar needed; following a set of instructions to load a new computer programme; searching the Internet for the best deals on flights to our chosen holiday location. Non-fiction reading forms an integral part of our daily lives.

Efficient readers modify the way they read according the nature of the text[7]. They will have a purpose when reading it - to answer a question or to find out more information. Reading non-fiction for a purpose is crucial – the reader has to be able to ask 'what do I want to get from this book, and why?'. That does not mean reading non-fiction is not pleasurable. A young child who loves dinosaurs will be motivated to read a book about prehistoric animals simply because of that interest. Likewise, reading a good story can lead the reader to want to explore the real-life setting or events that provided the stimulus for the plot. However, there are clear differences between story books and books predominantly written for information, and they need to be taught differently.

Whilst not a definitive list, it is generally agreed that there are six main non-fiction purposes or 'genre' types[8]:

- to recount or retell an event

- to report or describe something

- to instruct or to describe a procedure

- to explain how things work or how they came to be

- to discuss a particular issue, acknowledging different points of view

- to persuade the reader towards a particular position upheld by the writer.

In the Early and Transitional Stages of Cambridge Reading Adventures, authors wrote specifically for these purposes, enabling teachers to present one type of genre at a time, very clearly, and to teach the structural organisation and language features which support that purpose for reading. (See the table on page 15.)

Whilst non-fiction texts in the Conventional Stage follow the same language structures and text features as those in the earlier stages (such as use of labels and captions, fact boxes, maps and diagrams), most of the non-fiction books featured employ a range of different text types according to purpose. For example, a non-chronological report about diving can be interspersed with an explanation of how pearls are formed, and a persuasive text considering the importance of conservation.

Diving Under the Waves

[7] Wray, D. and Lewis, M. (1997). Extending Literacy: Children Reading and Writing Non-fiction. London, UK: Routledge.

[8] Bodman, S. and Franklin, G. (2014). Which Book and Why Using Book Bands and Book Levels for Guided Reading in Key Stage 1. London: IoE Press.

As reading progresses, readers will begin to encounter subject matter less familiar to them. Teachers will choose texts for guided reading predominantly according to the purpose for reading. However, they will also be considering the child's interests and exploiting their prior knowledge when approaching a new, unfamiliar subject. Good book choice is essential. As well as new subject matter, non-fiction texts will offer challenge in the grammatical structures and technical vocabulary choices used to convey the information. The teaching notes at the back of each book offer support for teaching non-fiction reading effectively. They provide links to the wider curriculum, ensuring that the books are used for a valid purpose. Guidance is provided to help teachers decide on the appropriate book to meet the needs of their group. Follow-up suggestions provide activities designed to develop non-fiction reading skills. Many of these are exemplified on the accompanying activity sheets.

Recount	• A sequence of events written in chronological order	• Written in the first (I/we) or third (he/she/they) person • Past tense verbs to indicate the event being retold has already occurred • The sequence of events is indicated by temporal connectives (first, next, later).
Report	• Commonly non-chronological: the sequence is determined by the component parts.	• Written in the present tense • Addresses the subject generically – not about specific things or people.
Instruction	• Chronologically sequenced steps, sometimes numbered. • May include diagrams	• Uses imperative verbs • Addresses the general reader • May include language of sequence (first, then, after that)
Explanation	• Steps organised in a logical sequence to explain or describe the process • Often use diagrams and cycles	• Written in the present tense • Temporal and causal connectives (because, in order to) used
Discussion	• Presents differing points of view • Draws a conclusion based on the argument presented.	• Written in the present tense • Connectives link the points being made (however, therefore). • Addresses the reader more generally
Persuasion	• Clear statement of the concern to be addressed • Logically sequence leading to a conclusion	• Written in the present tense • Use of powerful, often emotive language to put over the point of view

Teaching Reading

An Introduction to Cambridge Reading Adventures Strand Readers

Cambridge Reading Adventures comprises three stages: Early, Transitional and Conventional. There are Teaching and Assessment Guides provided at each stage.

Effective teaching in guided reading needs to offer materials with the right amount of challenge. Books at the Early and Transitional stages are organised into Book Bands[9] to provide a gradient of challenge for beginner readers. *Please see the Early and Transitional Teaching and Assessment Guides for detailed information about using Book Bands for guided reading, and assessment using banding for children learning to read.*

Once children are able to process a wide range of language structures, can decode fluently and are able to extract meaning from text, banding becomes no longer appropriate. This is because the elements that make a text challenging become far more nuanced; familiarity with the context, social and historical setting begin to exert a greater influence than in texts for learners between four and eight years old.

What are 'Strands'?

Guided reading books written for seven to twelve year olds bring a different set of considerations than those for young beginner readers. Books at the Conventional stage are arranged in strands that reflect the notion of reading as an adventure for young readers. Strands provide a different, more appropriate way to help evaluate text progression.

Children have learned the basic skills of reading, and are now ready to use those reading skills to learn. At this point in a child's reading progress, most words can be easily decoded, even complex, unfamiliar multisyllabic words. Books for seven to twelve year olds need to provide the environment in which to become fluent with a range of wider reading skills, as the nature of reading instruction in school changes.

The young reader now needs to apply these acquired word reading skills to an ever-increasing range of content and complexity: in the way characters are portrayed; in the lessening use of illustration to support the story line; in the length and complex structure of sentences. Content matter becomes less familiar and vocabulary increasing challenging. No reader ever stops using word reading skills. When we are reading a text book, for example, and come across words we do not know (such as 'stratigraphic' or 'nomenclature'), we use phonic and morphemic knowledge to sound out and chunk. We can read the words, even though we may not know what they mean. These are the challenges for the developing reader: 'The ability to comprehend text ... is a skill that will continue to develop throughout adult life'[10].

The challenges at the Conventional Stage of reading relate far more to the accessibility of context and subject, literary and language features, grammatical structures and vocabulary. Longer stories with multiple events, occurring over time, and with complex character relationships, require sustained concentration for extended periods. Gaining meaning of the text as a whole (text coherence) requires the reader to make inferential links using semantic and syntactic features. For example, in this line for 'A Tale of Two Sinbads' (Explorers – Strand 3):

The king '... held a great feast in Sinbad's honour and

invited Sinbad and **his** crew to join **him**.'

the reader has to know that 'his' refers to Sinbad and 'him' refers to the king. This type of inferential reading cannot be taken for granted.

---

[9] Bodman, S. and Franklin, G. (2014). *Which Book and Why: Using Book Bands and book levels for guided reading in Key Stage 1*. London: IOE Press

[10] Oakhill, J., Cain, K. and Elbro, C. (2015). Understanding and Teaching Comprehension: A Handbook. London: Routledge, p.4.

Authors also employ structural techniques such as chapters, headings and flashbacks to shape the book and support the reader through the story. All these areas of challenge interact to influence the position of a book in a particular strand.

Curriculum Links

The strands also take into account the requirements of any given curriculum for the reader at a specific point in their learning. Attention has been paid to age-related programmes of study, using the English National Curriculum and the Cambridge Assessment International Education Primary English Curriculum Framework, to ensure that books address teaching and learning needs in whatever context. A variety of fiction and non-fiction texts provide coverage of topics and subjects commonly covered in the school curriculum, such as the environment, travel and technology. As well as stories, books within the strands include myths and legends, poetry and playscripts, all appropriate to the curriculum expectations for the average age group. Authors have noted the requirements for grammar and vocabulary knowledge, and ample opportunity is provided in the texts for teachers to teach for increasing sentence complexity and to explore new more challenging words through supportive contexts and appropriate themes.

Strand Progression

Pathfinders – Strand 1	Age 7–8 approx. G3-G4
Wayfarers – Strand 2	Age 8–9 approx. G4-G5
Explorers – Strand 3	Age 9–10 approx. G5-G6
Voyagers – Strand 4	Age 10–12 approx. G6-G8

Choosing the right book

Text challenge at each strand is aimed at the average level for each age group. However, teachers have flexibility of choice. Use of the

assessments (in Section 3 of this Teaching and Assessment Guide) will help place children in an appropriate strand. The books are not confined to use in a specific year group but the reading attainment with a year group is the point of reference; books for 7–8, 8–9, 9–10 and 10–12 year olds. For higher attaining children, teachers can choose books from the year group above. Some children may still require the support of a banded system if they are not yet working at the expected standard for the 7–8 age group until the end of the year or into the next.

The wide variety of subjects and text types throughout the Conventional Stage also enables teachers to follow children's interests and motivation. A child fascinated by space travel, for example, may be motivated to read 'Journey to Callisto' with a more able friend, even if not reading at Strand 3 themselves. This makes the books at this strand a very flexible resource for teachers.

Teaching Reading

Using Strands to support children learning in an additional language

Many children reading Cambridge Reading Adventures will be learning English as an additional language. Many will be bilingual or multilingual. For others, English may be a new medium of learning. Being able to think, talk, read and write in more than one language is a real bonus in today's global society. However, learning to read in an additional language can present particular challenges. Languages employ different grammatical structures, such as the position of the verb in the sentence, the use of personal pronouns (she, he, it, in English) and how a question is formulated. Sometimes words have more than one meaning (the word 'post' can be applied to posting a letter, posting something on the internet, or something to which you tie a donkey). Words spelled the same but pronounced differently (such as 'read') rely on grammatical knowledge to fully comprehend the meaning: for example: 'I have read this book. Would you like to read it now?' - same word but two different pronunciations and grammatical purposes. Other words, such as 'wave', rely on understanding of the context to decide whether someone is at the beach, looking at the sea, or saying goodbye to someone. Idiomatic language does not directly translate - the English term 'raining cats and dogs' (meaning it is raining very heavily) may mean very little in a direct translation to a learner of English, without the cultural knowledge to support.

Cambridge Reading Adventures supports second language learning in a number of ways:

- Texts provide a good model of English to support the second language learner to hear, practise, and then predict and use in their own reading and writing;

- Challenges are carefully phased in order to ensure success and comprehension throughout all reading lessons;

- Vocabulary is supported by clear illustrations in both fiction and non-fiction texts;

- Choice of new and unfamiliar vocabulary is carefully considered to ensure that the reader is able to employ a range of word problem-reading skills, including decoding and syllabification (chunking), as well as use of meaning and sentence structure to successfully problem-solve;

- Links to the wider curriculum are made so that vocabulary and language structures encountered in reading can be reinforced in other subject study;

- Guidance for the teacher ensures that language and reading comprehension are at the heart of every guided reading lesson.

What is Guided Reading?

Guided reading is a teaching methodology; a way of organising teaching and assessment. It has specific goals. The teacher aims to support the children in reading text for themselves, putting into practice all the aspects of word and letter learning and reading strategies that have been taught previously. To do this, the teacher organises the class into small groups. For readers aged seven to twelve, each group is carefully matched to a strand through assessment. The teacher has a specific learning objective for the group and carefully chooses a book which will help address that objective; one that helps her guide the learning and thinking of the children in that group. The book offers some challenge to the readers and, by using awareness of the children's knowledge and experience, careful preparation of the text and the process of literacy acquisition, the teacher offers the right level of support to enable all the children to read the text independently. Active participation at each child's own level of attainment is the aim of guided reading.

A guided reading lesson has some key features:

- Small groups, usually between 4 to 8;
- Similar level of attainment in the group;
- A copy of the text for each child and the teacher;
- An unseen text in each guided reading lesson (often reading different sections of the same book over several lessons);
- Reading strategies are applied, reinforced and extended;
- The text can be accessed easily (at or above 90% accuracy);
- The children read independently whilst the teacher works with each individual child in turn (as opposed to reading aloud around the group);
- Teacher interactions focus on prompts and praise to support problem solving;
- The lessons follow a guided learning structure.

The Guided Reading Teaching Sequence

The guided reading lesson sequence creates:

- an opportunity for the teacher to teach reading strategies explicitly at a text level appropriate to each child.
- an effective and efficient way to provide instruction differentiated teaching to the range of attainment in a class.
- the opportunity for independent reading practice on the right levels of text for each child.
- a context to use and reinforce text, genre and metacognitive strategies being taught as part of a classroom literacy programme, resulting in systematic teaching.
- a focus on reading comprehension.

The table on page 20 gives an overview of the generic teaching sequence for guided reading. All guided reading lessons follow this structure, whether the children are well advanced in the process of learning to read or just beginning to learn. The emphasis and content of part of the sequence will be shaped to support the learner, whatever their current competences.

Teaching Reading

The essential elements of a guided reading lesson[11]

Before reading	Book introduction	**Lesson focus:** The teacher shares her learning objectives for the session with the children.
		Orientation: The teacher reads the title and gives a very brief overview of the text, particularly drawing attention to the type of text, clarifying the teaching objectives and building expectation.
		Preparation: Briefly, the teacher will 'debug' the book, alerting children's attention to any new features or challenges. Inexperienced readers will need more detailed introductions than competent readers. It is important to leave a certain amount of challenge. Children are encouraged to ask questions and make comments about the text. The aim is for each child to be able to read the text independently.
	Strategy check	The 'strategy check' prepares the children for independent reading and to provide opportunities to rehearse and practise the appropriate reading strategies they will need to employ to meet the challenges in the text.
		The teacher will prompt children to articulate what they will do if they become stuck whilst reading. This is about how they will attempt to solve their problem for themselves.
		Over time, and linked to the focus for teaching, teachers select different skills to focus on during the strategy check. One focus may last for a number of lessons.
During reading	Independent reading	Each child then reads independently. This is not a 'round robin' activity, with children taking turns to read while others listen. Maximum time is given to each child reading independently – the book introduction will have prepared him to meet the challenges this book has for him.
		The teacher listens in to first one child, then the next, monitoring and supporting where necessary. The teacher may have a rationale for which child she goes to first or leaves until last.
		The teacher's role in guided reading is to prompt a child to use print information, together with prior knowledge, and related to the teaching focus. Prompts and confirmation of useful responses provide a feedback mechanism for the child to realise their own success and keep track of their own progress in reading.
		This is also a time for the teacher to consider her assessment of each child's reading ability. Is the text at the right level for this child? Is there a suitable level of challenge?
After reading	Return to text	After this independent first reading, the teacher works with the whole group to reinforce the lesson focus. She will take children back to specific parts of the text to reinforce successful word reading or problem-solving or to reinforce an aspect that the children still found challenging. They are asked to share their successes and justify their responses. They may frame questions for each other arising from the text.
	Independent activity	An independent task may follow the reading. Teachers design activities that focus explicitly on the reasons for choosing that text: the learning objective.
		Reading independently from texts well within the child's current reading ability can also be used as an activity after a guided reading lesson. If resources allow, books that have been read will be placed in a 'book basket' or 'book box'. There will be one such collection for each reading group. These can be re-read independently following subsequent guided reading lessons, they can form the basis of free choice activities or be read to classmates or other adults at other times of the day.

[11] Bodman, S. and Franklin, G. (2014). *Which Book and Why: Using Book Bands and book levels for guided reading in Key Stage 1*. London: IOE Press, pp25-26.

Guided Reading Record Sheet

Class: Group:

Names:	Date: Text: Strand:
Key Learning Goals for the lesson:	
Learning Objective and Success Criteria	
Planning notes/Key questions/Comments	

Child	Notes and observations

Pathfinders - Strand 1 Characteristics

Books at the Pathfinders Strand reflect the growing maturity of the learner. Children are able to read books at an age-appropriate interest level. Their reading is accurate, fast and fluent to support comprehension. New and unfamiliar words can decoded and read. Vocabulary is developing through wider breadth and depth of reading.

Fiction

Events have a clear message, allowing the young reader to begin to make strong connections between the books and their own personal experiences, and to empathise with others. A greater range of literary devices to convey emotion begins to emerge. Children are starting to justify their point of view about what they have read, with support from the teacher.

Time and setting clearly demonstrated.

Longer, more complex sentences require meaning sustained over multiple clauses.

Precise meaning is indicated by choice of vocabulary.

Adverbs and adverbial phrases indicate character feeling and motivation.

Early the next morning, they met Agus, their guide, at the foot of the mountain.

'Mount Merapi can be very dangerous,' he explained. 'We need to take care to stick together, otherwise you can get lost or hurt yourself. There will be no one to help you up there. And remember, this is an active volcano. There have been one or two small tremors recently. If I say we have to turn back, we do exactly that!'

'Yes, of course,' said Jun. 'But I'm going to be first to the top,' she muttered to herself.

4

After an hour of climbing, Jun had already pushed her way to the front of the group. Daniel and Rafi jogged after her, reluctantly.

'Remember, it's an *experience*,' Rafi cried.

'Yeah – I want to experience being first up the mountain,' laughed Jun.

'Hey, you at the front, please slow down,' Agus cried. 'I must be able to see you at all times. Climbing Mount Merapi is very risky. Your life is in my hands.'

5

The Mountain of Fire, pages 4-5

Texts support strong characterisation.

Layout and paragraph breaks support reading comprehension.

Greater range of verbs give more precise meaning.

Chains of cause and effect are established to evidence conclusions drawn.

Non-fiction

Information books provide a secure model of genre style and presentation to allow links with writing to be forged as children enter the Conventional Reader stage. Familiar genre types such as instructional and non-chronological report texts are becoming more complex. The content featured is age-appropriate for seven to eight year olds.

Sentences have two or three clauses, with a greater range of connectives used.

Texts provide strong and consistent examples of the genre.

Toto learns from Honey

Toto watched his mother. He was always ready to follow her wherever she went. By the time that Toto was four months old, he could run away from danger. But he needed his mother to warn him when danger was coming. Toto was still very small.

Honey spent hours staring across the plains. She had to be ready for anything. She liked to go as high up as she could. She would choose a small mound, so that she could see everything around her.

Fact Box
Cheetahs cannot climb trees well. They must rely on their speed and skill to get out of danger.

Cheetahs can also hear the smallest sound.

Like all cheetahs, Honey has very good eyesight during the day, but she does not see well at night.

16

17

Honey and Toto, pages 16-17

Text organisation supports the purpose and authorial intent.

Mixed genre as appropriate – for example report and recount.

Books use a widening range of layout and writing styles to convey information.

Children at this strand will be reading a range of appropriate texts fluently and accurately. Teachers will be supporting reading for comprehension. Texts integrate a dialogue alongside literary language and language designed for strong impact on reading comprehension. Children working at this band will be reading beyond the 'words on the page' and levels of inferential reading will be greater than previously required.

Fiction

Whilst reading stories, children will draw on the text to infer characters' feelings, thoughts and motives from their actions, justifying their inferences with evidence. Fiction books are likely to contain chapters to reflect the sustained reading of one book over a period of time.

The sentence construction draws attention to important meaning in the text.	The construction of paragraphs is becoming more sophisticated.	Sentences are increasingly complex, with strong structures to support comprehension.

He got the levers into position, pressed the ignition button and the digger started up. Yash knew exactly what to do. He pulled some of the levers and pushed others, and suddenly the digger began to move slowly forward.

'So far, so good' said Yash.

He pulled and pushed other levers, and the digger began to turn to the right as it moved. Then Yash put it into reverse, and, finally, brought it to a stop.

'Very good,' He said. 'Looks like you've fixed it.'

'Can I have a go?' asked Dak.

Yash moved along the driver's seat to make room for Dak to sit next to him, and then, as the digger moved slowly, he talked Dak through how to move the digger forward and backwards, and turning left and right.

'How am I doing?' asked Dak.

'Not bad, at all,' smiled Yash. He pressed the button to turn off the engine. 'Let's save the diesel. We'll practise some more tomorrow.'

The Digger, pages 20-21

Illustrations support the inference required.	Strong story lines that evoke character motive and intent.	Clear reasons for chapter breaks, such as to signal a new event, are evident.

Non-fiction

Children will be developing their knowledge and skills of reading non-fiction across a range of subjects, linked to the classroom curriculum and their own interests. Readers are beginning to notice how information is portrayed and to justify their understanding with reference to the text.

Reading new, unfamiliar words is supported by sentence structure and spelling patterns.

Children can discuss and suggest reasons for differences in text organisation.

Text layout is organised appropriately, according to purpose, allowing children to evaluate how effectively information is provided.

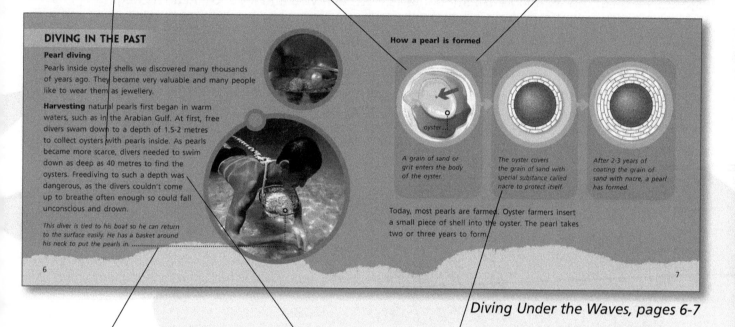

DIVING IN THE PAST

Pearl diving

Pearls inside oyster shells we discovered many thousands of years ago. They became very valuable and many people like to wear them as jewellery.

Harvesting natural pearls first began in warm waters, such as in the Arabian Gulf. At first, free divers swam down to a depth of 1.5-2 metres to collect oysters with pearls inside. As pearls became more scarce, divers needed to swim down as deep as 40 metres to find the oysters. Freediving to such a depth was dangerous, as the divers couldn't come up to breathe often enough so could fall unconscious and drown.

This diver is tied to his boat so he can return to the surface easily. He has a basket around his neck to put the pearls in. ....

How a pearl is formed

oyster...

A grain of sand or grit enters the body of the oyster.

The oyster covers the grain of sand with special substance called nacre to protect itself.

After 2-3 years of coating the grain of sand with nacre, a pearl has formed.

Today, most pearls are farmed. Oyster farmers insert a small piece of shell into the oyster. The pearl takes two or three years to form.

6

7

Diving Under the Waves, pages 6-7

Books employ a range of text features appropriate to the subject matter and the age of the children.

Complex sentences are demarcated accurately to aid reading for comprehension.

Comprehension is developing, and texts allow children to analyse word meaning in context.

Children reading within the Explorers Strand, will be reading a wider range of material, both fiction and non-fiction, with a good degree of accuracy and at a reasonable reading pace. They will be mostly reading silently unless the task calls for reading aloud (such as playscripts or performance poetry, for example). Reading in class may well take the form of literature circles to discuss independent reading for comprehension. Children will be able to express their reading preferences, and to read critically, considering the author's effectiveness in addressing audience and purpose (word choice, grammatical structure, layout, etc).

Fiction

Fiction books are written in chapters to provide practice in sustaining comprehension across one book over a short period of time. Story structures are clear so children are aware of sequencing occurring over time. Characters are strong and clearly defined. Real-life adventure stories are balanced with more traditional tales, such as myths and legends. Readers begin to recognise how their response to text is shaped by the author's viewpoint and their own experiences.

Language and vocabulary choices are appropriate to the story style.

Readers interpret author intent through context clues rather than being told explicitly.

Character trait is often implied rather than overtly stated.

CHAPTER ONE
Sinbad the Sailor returns home

The city of Baghdad was just beginning to wake. The river sparkled in the morning light as the sun rose. A tall, handsome man stood alone on the deck of a sailing ship, admiring what he saw. He had been away travelling for three long years and had had many adventures. At last he was back in the city where he was born.

2

This man was Sinbad the Sailor, one of the richest and most famous travellers in the world. But you would not have known it to look at him. When he went away, a great crowd of people had come to wave him goodbye. But now, there was nobody to welcome him home.

'Nobody knows I am here,' he told himself. 'Everyone thinks I'm dead or that I've gone away forever.' He ran his fingers through his bushy beard and looked down at his dirty clothes. 'I need to go home, have a bath and change into clean clothes,' he thought.

Suddenly he had an idea. What fun it would be to keep secret the fact that he was alive! He could wander the streets like a stranger. Perhaps he would find out if anyone still remembered him.

3

A Tale of Two Sinbads, pages 2-3

The author clearly shapes the setting and characterisation.

Longer sentences include adverbial clauses to add detail and support comprehension.

Readers have opportunity to predict from text and knowledge of the story type.

Non-fiction

Non-fiction books will contain all features seen at earlier stages of Cambridge Reading Adventures. Many texts will have sections which follow a different genre style or presentation to the main text – a brief recount within a report for example.

Aspects of argument and persuasion will be used in an age-appropriate context and setting, such as in considering renewable resources and wild-life conservation. Different perspectives are demonstrated, and children are encouraged to read critically, acknowledging the difference between fact and opinion, and to question across different sources.

Evidence of both fact and opinion in non-fiction texts.

Vocabulary choices and language structure reinforce the message given.

Books acknowledge that non-fiction does not necessarily contain the 'right' answers.

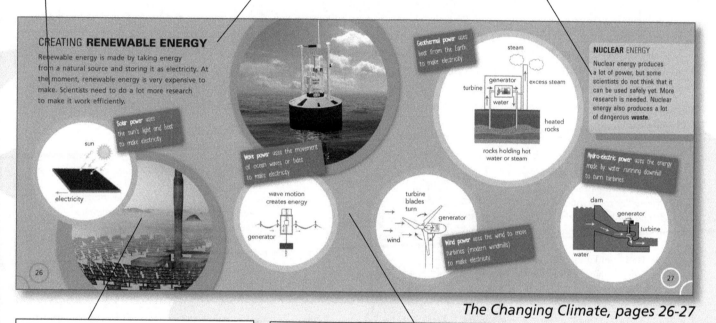

The Changing Climate, pages 26-27

Appropriate layout and design features for the genre.

Presentation aids retrieving, recording and presenting of information on a given topic.

Voyagers - Strand 4 Characteristics

By the end of primary school, the reader is experienced at handling a range of genre and is able to discuss how language is used and how vocabulary choice causes reactions and inferences in the reader. Texts have literary/technical language as appropriate to the particular text, such as more archaic or poetic language in historical stories.

Across the Voyager Strand, texts use writing devices such as flashbacks, summary and commentary. Stories are longer, in the form of a short novel, played out over time and including a range of characters. Topics reflect real-life experiences, such as overcoming disability or disadvantage.

Fiction

Fiction books in this series contain chapters to reflect the sustained reading in one book over a short period of time. Books provide good opportunities to analyse the success of the writers' craft in evoking particular responses in the reader, for example, where we feel sorry for a character with flaws.

Narrative structure techniques, such as flashbacks, enable the story to be told from different perspectives.

New chapters signal a change in time, place and events as appropriate.

Emotive language influences how the reader interprets authorial intent.

And then the war came. Bombs raining down on the city, whole streets destroyed. Ahmed's father had been working at the hospital, carrying out an operation, when it had been hit. He'd been killed, along with other doctors and nurses, and patients.

Then their house had been hit, as were many others. Lots of their neighbours had been killed.

'We will die if we stay here,' said his mother.

So they'd packed some essential things and joined the hundreds of people fleeing the city and heading for the nearest border.

And here they were, with their previous life just a memory. Just waiting. But for how long?

18

Chapter 3

After the incident with the rice, Ahmed did his best to keep away from Bozan. If he saw Bozan walking down one of the streets, he went by another route to avoid him. Once, he was horrified to see Bozan actually hanging around outside his family's tent. Ahmed's mother also saw him and went out to ask what he wanted, but Bozan said nothing, and just walked away.

Ahmed told his friends, Mustafa and Mezut, about what had happened over the rice, and the old man coming to his rescue. But he didn't tell them about Bozan crying. It didn't seem right to tell them.

'At least you won't have to see Bozan any time soon,' said Mezut. 'We haven't got another game for a couple of weeks, and that's against Sandy City, and they're younger than us.'

But, as it turned out, Ahmed would be seeing Bozan a lot sooner than expected.

19

The Refugee Camp, pages 18-19

Varying sentence lengths are used to build tension and engage the reader.

Character is built up as events occur, and motives and actions change accordingly.

Texts require the reader to infer motive, and explain their views to others.

Non-fiction

Non-fiction books will contain all features seen at the Transitional stage. Texts have become less 'obvious' and distinct in use of genre features. Predominantly, a mixed genre approach is used, as appropriate, for example a historical recount within an explanatory text. Vocabulary choices are authentic and relate to the subject matter. Content seeks to provoke a response and challenge the reader. Opportunities to make links with the school curriculum and culture are provided.

> Sufficient depth to support analytic discussions of the text.

> Word choices seek to position the reader.

> Careful consideration of design and layout as appropriate to text purpose.

Anime: Japan's Fantastic Cartoon Makers

Japanese animation, called Anime in Japan, is as old as the film industry. Starting as far back as the early 1900's, the oldest surviving Anime is 'Namakura Gatana', meaning Blunt Sword. Japanese animators like fast-paced action and **fantastical** characters. They can also portray very touching stories where children find ways to overcome **adversity**.

One beautifully animated films is 'My Neighbour Totoro' released in 1988. Like most films made by Miyazaki's Studio Ghibli, this family film has a powerful **ecological** theme.

Japanese Anime continues to produce outstanding animations that transport the audience to amazing places and tell wonderfully imaginative stories.

Anime is very stylised. For example, characters have bigger eyes than usual. This allows for many emotions to be shown clearly through the eyes.

FILM FACTS
Animated 'shorts', as they are called, only last a few minutes but feature length movies and animation can last up to two hours.

Tortoro and Satsuki wait for the bus in the rain in a scene from 'My Neighbour Totoro'.

12

an example of Anime's style of animation

13

Movie World, pages 12-13

> Content is seeking to challenge the reader to read beyond the text and make connections with wider issues.

> All non-fiction text features are used as appropriate to convey the message.

> Word choices are authentic and relate to the subject.

Book Review—Fiction

Book Title _____

Author _____

Illustrator _____

Who are the main characters in the story?

Write a short summary of the story.

What did you like about the story? Explain why.

Was there anything you didn't like? Explain why.

Would you recommend this book to a friend? Explain why.

How many stars would you award this book? Colour in the number of stars.

☆　☆　☆　☆　☆

Book Review—Non-fiction

Book Title _____

Author _____

Photographer _____

Genre _____

What is this book about? Write a short summary.

What did you like about the non-fiction text? Explain why.

Was there anything you didn't like? Explain why.

Would you recommend this book to a friend? Explain why.

How many stars would you award this book? Colour in the number of stars.

☆ ☆ ☆ ☆ ☆

Story Tracker

Book Title _____

Author _____

Illustrator _____

Main characters

Setting

Problem

Conflict

Climax

Resolution

Reading Log

Book Title _____

Author _____

Make notes in your reading log as you read this book.

What were your first impressions of this book?

Part-way through—how do you feel about the book now?

Did the ending surprise you?

Would you have ended the story in a different way?

Write down any new and exciting words you learned whilst reading this book.

What will you read next? Would you like to read another book by this author? Or a book on the same subject? Explain why.

Teaching Reading

Reading independently

What is independent reading?

Think for a moment about your own personal experiences of reading: excitement waiting for the next book in the series to come out, perhaps, or the time when a friend recommended a book that you really enjoyed. Maybe you belong to a book group, or enjoy sharing reading experiences online through social media. As a reader, you make decisions for yourself about what to read, when to read and how to read. You are reading independently. Independent readers are motivated to read. They chose to read of their own free will and have an expectation that the reading will be pleasurable.

Cremin et al. (2014)[12] describe reading for pleasure as a transformational act, one in which participants see and value themselves as readers. Reading changes lives. Research evidence points to a link between reading frequency, reading ability and the desire to read.[13] Just as we don't improve our breaststroke by sitting on the edge of a pool watching others swim, so the more we read, the better we become at reading.

Teachers play a crucial role in supporting and developing the independent reader. It is important that the texts children chose to read independently are easy to read within their current reading capability. This starts with the guided reading lesson. By introducing the text first in the lesson, teachers prepare children to be able to read the book by themselves. Teachers make appropriate book choices, address the challenges and teach for the reading skills needed to make this text accessible. This approach will support reading independently on this text and help develop the skills and strategies needed for reading unfamiliar texts independently.

Opportunities to read independently will also take place at home. Children read aloud to a parent or carer in the early stages of learning to read. Later, reading may be a quiet, personal activity. Reading at home needs to be a pleasurable experience. Books sent home from school should be easy and enjoyable. Cambridge Reading Adventures provides a guide leaflet to help parents support reading at home.

Organising a reading library

What do we mean by a 'reading library'? In the context of reading independently, we define this as a place where children can spend time reading, browsing and choosing books. In some schools, this may be in the classroom. In others, there may be a designated room or space. Many schools will have both. We also acknowledge that there will be books and resources specifically for teaching purposes which may be stored separately in a teaching resource room.

The library is the focal point of any school's reading provision. It is the place where reading for pleasure is promoted. The library should be the responsibility of all staff. A good, well-provisioned, busy and welcoming library demonstrates to all the value placed on engendering a love of reading.

Schools will need to give careful consideration to address the progression of reading for seven to twelve year olds. Books should be accessible, and children coming to the library should be able to easily locate something they want to read. Books could be arranged in suitability for different ages, or grouped according to topics. In the Conventional Stage of Cambridge Reading Adventures books have been placed in strands according to the complexity of subject and theme, grammatical structures, plot development and linguistic challenge. The Strand Overviews in this guide (pages 22-29) can be useful to apply a general gradient of text challenge to existing and new books in the school library.

It is also important to provide a range of fiction and non-fiction genres to address children's interests and related to the school curriculum. Cambridge Reading Adventures includes:

- short stories
- longer chapter books
- books in series (the International School stories)
- myths and legends
- adventure stories
- poetry
- plays
- non-fiction texts covering the six text types (see p 15).

[12] Cremin, T., Mottram, M., Collins, F., Powell, S. and Safford, K. (2014). Building Communities of Engaged Readers: Reading for Pleasure. London: Routledge.

[13] Clark, C. and Douglas, J. (2011) Young People's Reading and Writing: An in-depth study focusing on enjoyment, behaviour, attitudes and attainment. London: National Literacy Trust

Afterwards, she sat with her friends as they drank their orange juice. They had lost the game. Everyone seemed sad and tired. Leila tried to cheer them up but it was no use. Leila knew there had to be a reason why her friends hadn't won the game. If only she could think of a way to help them start winning.

Leila turned to her best friend, Zara.
'Hard luck Zara,' she said, 'I thought you all played really well.'

'Thanks Leila,' replied Zara. 'I am disappointed, but thanks for the great support. You cheered louder than anyone.'

Leila's Game, like all the international school stories, encourages the readers to empathise with a range of characters.

Literacy learning in the classroom

Guided reading is one element of a rich reading provision. As discussed previously, teachers will use whole class shared teaching to demonstrate and model how reading works, and will provide opportunities for children to read independently or with a partner in paired reading to practise and apply what has been taught. Using this variety of teaching learning opportunities, teachers can support the progression of reading skills, extend grammar and vocabulary knowledge, develop reading for comprehension and address learning outcomes in a purposeful way through reading.

Reading supports writing. Most writers are also avid readers. As we read, we notice interesting words and phrases. We encounter new vocabulary, and spot interesting spelling patterns. We are drawn into the story by the author's clever use of sentence structure and we are kept engaged in the plot by the use of cliff-hangers and page turners. We like some characters, and can empathise with them. We think others are not so nice and deserve their 'comeuppance' at the end. As we read, so we think about how we might use these ideas, techniques and strategies in our writing.

Cambridge Reading Adventures supports the development of literacy learning. Each book contains a guided reading lesson plan, with suggestions for developing spelling, grammar and vocabulary in group or whole class work. The activity sheets included in this guide provide independent activities to support both writing and comprehension.

Becoming a reader

Our aim as teachers of reading is that our children become motivated, engaged and critical readers - readers who gain satisfaction from the act of reading itself. Once children have mastered the art of learning to read, the challenge is to maintain the motivation - to become a life-long reader. In this process, the teacher acts as guide and as model within a whole school culture of reading: reading clubs, literature circles, vibrant libraries and time to read and to talk about reading.

Reading is a skill for life, and we never stop learning. It is indeed an Adventure!

SECTION 2: BOOK BY BOOK OVERVIEW

Title	Band	Fiction / Non-fiction
Four Clever Brothers	STRAND 1: Pathfinders	F
Honey and Toto: the story of a cheetah family	STRAND 1: Pathfinders	NF
River Rescue	STRAND 1: Pathfinders	F
Connections	STRAND 1: Pathfinders	NF
The Mountain of Fire	STRAND 1: Pathfinders	F
Leila's Game	STRAND 1: Pathfinders	F
Timbuktu	STRAND 2: Wayfarers	NF
The Digger	STRAND 2: Wayfarers	F
Diving Under The Waves	STRAND 2: Wayfarers	NF
The Mystery of Sol	STRAND 2: Wayfarers	F
You and Me	STRAND 2: Wayfarers	F
Who is the Greatest?	STRAND 2: Wayfarers	NF
A Tale of Two Sinbads	STRAND 3: Explorers	F
Dolphins in the Wild	STRAND 3: Explorers	NF
Journey to Callisto	STRAND 3: Explorers	NF
Skyscrapers	STRAND 3: Explorers	NF
The Changing Climate	STRAND 3: Explorers	NF
Hunters of the Sea	STRAND 3: Explorers	F
Movie World	STRAND 4: Voyagers	NF
The White Elephant	STRAND 4: Voyagers	F
Meltdown	STRAND 4: Voyagers	F
The Cave at the End of the World	STRAND 4: Voyagers	F
The Refugee Camp	STRAND 4: Voyagers	F
Tamerlane and the Boy	STRAND 4: Voyagers	F

Title: Four Clever Brothers
Author: Lynne Rickards

Strand 1 Pathfinders
Genre: Play

Overview

This playscript is designed to be read aloud during guided reading lessons. It features six characters so that each member of the group has a speaking part. The story follows a traditional style of retelling in which the wise brothers are able to prove to the judge that they are not thieves, and that they can help the camel owner recover his lost camel. Other traditional tales, such as Grimms' 'Four Skilful Brothers', or more recent versions such as 'The Three Brothers' by JK Rowling can offer opportunities for comparison.

Learning outcomes

Children can:

- recognise features of playscripts and comment on their effectiveness;

- use the grammar and language structure to support the decoding of complex or less familiar words;

- monitor how effective their oral reading sounds in conveying meaning to the listener.

Language structure

- Easily recognisable stylistic use of traditional language, such as: *'Tell me …'* on p.8 and *'Hear my plea!'* on p.12.

- Sentences may have two or three clauses and a greater range of connectives (see, for example, p.20).

Book structure/visual features

- The conventions of a playscript are followed, e.g. cast list, stage directions, dialogue layout.

- Clear layout of direct speech supports expression and oral delivery when reading aloud.

Vocabulary and comprehension

- Developing comprehension is supported through speech layout and punctuation.

- Statements, questions and exclamations are used to effectively demonstrate the meaning, and to uphold the stylistic devices, such as *'Tell me, is your camel blind in one eye?'* on p.8.

Curriculum links

Science – the brothers are very scientific in their explanation of the missing camel's whereabouts. Use non-fiction sources to explore different animal tracks. Look for evidence of animal or bird tracks in the local area. Make animal tracks in sand and clay for other children to guess what the animal might be.

Geography – Explore how real-life camels are used to support life in desert regions. The Cambridge Reading Adventures book 'Desert Life' (Gold Band) might be useful here.

Using the activity sheets

Reading Comprehension: The author has used the adjective 'clever' to describe the brothers to the reader. The activity helps children identify other words and phrases that describe the characters, and which aid expression when read aloud.

Writing Composition: As a follow-up activity, children could rewrite the play as a story, using third person narrative. The activity sheet provides a writing frame for this activity.

Reading Comprehension

The play is called 'Four Clever Brothers'. The author has used the word 'clever' to describe the brothers. This tells us something about them and helps us understand how to read the words of each character in the play.

This is Kamran. Find a word or phrase in the play that describes his character.

_____

Find something Kamran does or says in the play that shows his character.

_____

_____

This is Tazim. Find a word or phrase in the play that describes his character.

_____

Find something Tazim does or says in the play that shows his character.

_____

_____

This is Sadiq. Find a word or phrase in the play that describes his character.

_____

Find something Sadiq does or says in the play that shows his character.

_____

_____

This is Latif. Find a word or phrase in the play that describes his character.

_____

Find something Latif does or says in the play that shows his character.

_____

_____

Learning outcome:

How vocabulary choice supports reading aloud in play reading

Writing Composition

'Four Clever Brothers' is written as a playscript. Your job is to write it as a story.

Think about the words you might use to show how the characters are feeling, such as:

| SHOUTED | | CRIED | | THOUGHT |

What adjectives would describe the characters? Look at page 2 of the play to help you.

Here is how you could start your story ...

It was a hot day. Four brothers were walking along a dusty path. Suddenly they saw some footprints on the path.

Learning outcome:

To rewrite a playscript as a story

STRAND 1 Pathfinders

Title: Honey and Toto: the story of a cheetah family
Author: Jonathan and Angela Scott

Strand 1 Pathfinders
Genre: Non-fiction

Overview

This beautiful book features stunning real-life photography from the work of Jonathan and Angela Scott. The text is built around the pictures to tell the life of a young cheetah cub, Toto, and his mother, Honey, on the plains of the Masai Mara, in Kenya, Africa. Written in part as a recount, the Scotts tell their story directly to the reader, whilst additional information about cheetahs is provided through a variety of non-fiction features.

Learning outcomes

Children can:

- recognise the writing styles used in different text types, commenting on the effectiveness in conveying the author's message
- comment on how different purposes are reflected in more complex non-fiction texts
- read with accuracy and demonstrate understanding by responding to questions.

Language structure

- Clear examples of the structures appropriate to the genre are provided, such as the use of personal voice: '*We called the mother cheetah 'Honey'* (p.2) and present tense, generic report style: '*Cheetahs can run at 70 miles per hour*' (p.5).
- Captions are written in the present tense (for example: '*Toto knows he must hide quickly.*' on p.19), engaging the reader in the action.

Book structure/visual features

- Purpose and audience is clearly supported by text organization and layout.
- There is a variety of appropriate non-fiction layout features employed.

Vocabulary and comprehension

- Subject-specific vocabulary relates to the topic and content of the book.
- Longer, multisyllabic words provide opportunity to rehearse word-reading skills.

Curriculum links

Science – Use information texts and the Internet to find out more about cheetahs.

Literacy – Research other wild-life writers who have chronicled their life with animals. Look at the writing style used in recounting their experiences.

Using the activity sheets

Reading Comprehension: In guided reading, children have been finding answers to questions posed. The comprehension activity sheet provides more opportunity to demonstrate understanding by responding to questions.

Writing Composition: Use the activity sheet to reinforce the different non-fiction text features used in the book, asking the children to write captions of their own.

Reading Comprehension

Read pages 8 and 9 in 'Honey and Toto'. Now answer these questions. Write in complete sentences.

Question:

Why do scientists think cheetahs have black tear marks?

Your answer:

41

Question:

What do you think 'full of life' means?

Your answer:

Question:

Why did Toto need to stay hidden?

Your answer:

Now write a question of your own for your friend to answer:

Your question:

Learning outcome:

Demonstrate understanding by responding to questions

Writing composition

'Honey and Toto' is a non-fiction book. It uses lots of non-fiction text features to tell us about how cheetahs live.

Think about how the author used the non-fiction features here.

This caption tells us what is happening in the picture. Could you write a different caption for this picture?

Why is this information given in a Fact Box?

Why is this word in bold?

What does it mean?

Honey lived on her own for most of the time. She wandered over the grassy plains and woodlands, hunting gazelles and wildebeest and other smaller animals.

Fact Box
Cheetahs can run at 70 miles per hour.

Cheetahs cannot run fast for long. They must catch their prey quickly.

5

Now choose another page from the book, and write a new caption for the picture. Remember a caption is written as a complete sentence.

Page number ....

Caption:

Learning outcome:

Comment on the purpose and effectiveness of non-fiction text features

Title: River Rescue
Author: Peter Millett

Strand 1 Pathfinders
Genre: Fiction

Overview

This exciting story follows the adventures of Kamon and his father as they attempt to rescue two young boys stranded when a flash flood hits the river. Kamon's quick thinking saves the day. The story offers opportunities to consider multiple strands within the story line (for example, the interplay between the two different families) and causal effects, such as the implication of Kamon deciding to take his drone with him to the river.

Learning outcomes

Children can:

- recall the main episodes, ideas and events of the story, when reading the same text over more than one lesson

- use morphology-based strategies to recall the meaning of words new to them

- listen to how their reading sounds, and monitor for effective oral delivery of their reading.

Language structure

- Contractions are used in speech for emphasis, including those easily confused with words without an apostrophe (for example, *'I'll'* on p.3; *'we're'* on p.13).

- The position of the reporting clause varies, either within or at the end of the dialogue, depending on the length of the sentence and for authorial intent. See, for example: *'No,' said his father. 'There's not enough time.'* (p.9)

Book structure/visual features

- Short chapters provide breaks at key points in the story (*'cliff-hangers'*).

- paragraphing supports reading comprehension, for example by clearly delineating events as they occur (as on p.13).

Vocabulary and comprehension

- Subject-specific vocabulary is used (*kayak, drone, life jackets, flash flood*) and children will need to understand these terms as central to the plot.

- Character action is implied (such as how the two boys became stranded).

Curriculum links

Science – in a study of weather patterns and extreme weather incidents, this book provides an example of how flash floods can build quickly and cause devastation. Use the internet to investigate other flood disasters and what can be done to protect against them.

Using the activity sheets

Reading Comprehension: In guided reading, you will have explained use of a 'cliff hanger' to keep the reader engaged. The activity sheet helps children think about what might happen next.

Writing Composition: In this follow-up activity, children identify the key events in the story. You will have been preparing them for this in the discussion following the guided reading of 'River Rescue'.

Reading Comprehension

Read up to p.15. The author uses a 'cliff hanger' to keep us excited about what will happen next:

> "Just keep flying it,' Mr Pattama said. Kamon's idea is the best chance we have.'
>
> Will Kamon's drone be strong enough to carry the rope?
>
> Will it have enough battery left to reach the boys on the rocks?
>
> What do you think will happen next? Think of three ways the story might continue.

I think that …

Or that …

Or perhaps …

Learning outcome:

Use key events in the story to predict what happens next

Writing Composition

Story Map

Now you have finished reading 'River Rescue', complete the story map.

Who are the main characters? _____

Where does the story take place? _____

What is the problem?

What happens first?

What happens next?

What happens then?

How is the problem resolved?

Learning outcome:

Recall the main episodes, ideas and events of the story

Title: Connections
Author: Scoular Anderson

Strand 1 Pathfinders
Genre: Non-fiction

Overview

This beautifully illustrated book explores the path of human invention from the very first stone tools through to the microchips of today's computers.

Learning outcomes

Children can:

- consider how text structure and presentation supports comprehension
- identify changes in verb tense, and understand how this supports the chronology of events
- identify unknown words when reading, and use appropriate strategies to ascertain their meaning.

Language structure

- Appropriate grammatical structures are used, such as the impersonal voice and past tense verbs. ('*threads were woven into cloth*', p12. '*People have always needed help to work things out*', p.16).
- Adverbial words and phrases ('*About 60 years ago*', p.24; '*Now*', p.25) denote the sequence of events over time.
- Complex sentences are used, demarcated accurately (see p.3, for example)

Book structure/visual features

- Captioned illustrations provide additional information to aid comprehension of the main text.
- A clear logical structure, with additional non-fiction features such as a timeline (pp.28-29), supports the chronology.

Vocabulary and comprehension

- Clear, simple explanations of technical aspects are given, supported by illustrations (see, for example, p.24).

Curriculum links

History – The book could be used in various different historical topics, comparing aspects of life in different periods and supporting the chronology of change over time.

Computer Science – The book explains early calculating machines and developments in the binary system, which are key components of the information technology curriculum. Work on the binary code can lead to further study of coding, such as historical code-breakers, and the children designing their own codes.

Using the activity sheets

Reading Comprehension: Provide children with the activity sheet after lesson one to support them to identify unknown words in the text, and to think about what they might mean.

Writing Composition: Linked to a topic of study, children can use Scoular Anderson's design and layout to write about something they are learning in class, for example, in history. Refer also to his other books in the CRA series.

Reading Comprehension

'Connections' introduces lots of new vocabulary words. Find and write some you do not know.

Look at the text to see if you can work out what this word might mean. Write a definition. Now check with a dictionary – were you right?

Word

I think this word means

The dictionary says

Word

I think this word means

The dictionary says

Word

I think this word means

The dictionary says

Word

I think this word means

The dictionary says

Learning outcome:

Find the meaning of unknown words in text

Writing Composition

Scoular Anderson's books are drawn and written in a very specific style.

Look at how Scoular uses pictures, arrows and captions to design his work.

Use this sheet to design a page about something you are studying in class.

Learning outcome:

Use features of layout and design to write own non-fiction text

STRAND 1 Pathfinders

Title: The Mountain of Fire
Author: Peter Millett

Strand 1 Pathfinders
Genre: Fiction

Overview

Mount Merapi is an active volcano in Indonesia, and it provides the backdrop for this exciting adventure story. Character depictions are strong to support empathy and identification, whilst the subject matter reflects the growing maturity of the young reader at this strand.

Learning outcomes

Children can:

- express opinion about character and storyline, locating specific words and phrases to support their view
- recall the main episodes, ideas and events thematically rather than simple sequential retelling
- Explore personalized ways to remember the meaning and spelling of new words encountered in text.

Language structure

- The writing style is appropriate to an adventure story genre, such as when Agus makes his emergency call on p. 8: *'Emergency! [...] Repeat, emergency!'*
- Recording conventions of speech punctuation are used appropriately to support reading aloud with expression and characterisation.

Book structure/visual features

- Chapters are used effectively to build tension and suspense.
- The book is organised to support authorial purpose and intent, for example in the illustration depicting the characters' descent, to stress the danger on p.9.

Vocabulary and comprehension

- New, unfamiliar vocabulary is not directly supported by illustrations, requiring inferential reading to ensure meaning is established.
- Some examples of technical language within a fiction structure, such as *'molten'* and *'tremors'*.

Curriculum links

Science – Mount Merapi in Indonesia erupted most recently in 2010. There are other active volcanoes around the world. Use non-fiction and internet resources to explore volcanic eruptions and the impact on the surrounding communities. Why would people chose to live near active volcanoes?

Literacy – write explanation texts outlining what happens during a volcanic eruption.

Using the activity sheets

Reading Comprehension: In guided reading, you will have been drawing the children's attention to words and phrases which describe how the characters are thinking and feeling at the end of p.8. Demonstrate how to use the activity sheet to describe what Agus and Jun are feeling.

Writing Composition: At the end of the guided reading lesson, discuss how Jun might retell the event to her parents. Tell the children they will be pretending to be Jun. Would there be things she might not tell her parents?

Reading Comprehension

Read up to page 8. Think about the words and phrases the author has used to tell us how these characters might be feeling, such as:

| CRIED | 'RUN FOR YOUR LIVES!' | YELLED | FROWNED | RELUCTANTLY | MUMBLED |

Write in the speech bubble what each character might be thinking to themselves at at this point in the story.

JUN

AGUS

Learning outcome:

Give opinions about how characters are thinking and feeling, based on evidence from reading

Writing Composition

Jun's family are waiting for news – they will be worried about her.

Write an email in role as Jun explaining the event from her point of view.

Hi Mum and Dad,

Don't worry – I'm OK

Learning outcome:

Recall the main events thematically rather than as a simple sequential retelling.

Title: Leila's Game
Author: Spike Breakwell and Colin Millar

Strand 1 Pathfinders
Genre: Fiction

Overview

Leila is a familiar character from earlier books in the CRA International School strand. In this story, Leila is worried about her friends in the basketball team. They keep losing their games. A discussion with her grandfather gives her an idea, and she is able to help them plan a strategy using the strengths of each team member. The story tackles familiar themes of friendship and problem-solving, with a satisfying resolution.

Learning outcomes

Children can:

- note how dialogue is presented in a range of styles, such as using questions and exclamations, and with the reporting clause embedded (as, for example, on p.6, *'No,' agreed Leila. 'I can't understand it.'*), using these to aid reading and comprehension

- make sensible predictions, justifying these with evidence from the text and from prior knowledge

- hold story events in their heads during a reading lesson, learning to recall significant facts/ideas when reading the same text over more than one lesson.

Language structure

- The text provides clear layout of direct speech with punctuation to aid reading aloud with expression and meaning.

- Sentences are longer with two or three clauses, providing information about characters and events to support comprehension.

Book structure/visual features

- Story events are sustained over time and place, supported by chapter breaks and illustrations.

Vocabulary and comprehension

- New and specific vocabulary is introduced in a strong, supportive context, such as when Grandfather explains the meaning of a strategy to Leila on p.14.

- A variety of verbs is used in reporting clauses to conclude dialogue, e.g. 'smiled', 'asked', 'replied' on p.13.

Curriculum links

History – Backgammon is thought to be one of the oldest board games, at about 5,000 years old. Children could explore the history of board games played in their country.

Maths – Backgammon is played by rolling dice to decide on the moves each player makes. Explore the rules of probability with dice, for example what number combination will occur most in 20 rolls of the dice?

Using the activity sheets

Reading Comprehension: In the second guided reading lesson, children will discuss key events in the story. This activity sheet provides an opportunity for children to prepare for that lesson.

Writing Composition: As a follow-up activity, children can use the writing frame to write their own match report. Discuss how a match report is written, and look for words and phrases used in 'Leila's Game' that will help the children.

STRAND 1 Pathfinders

Reading Comprehension

Read chapters 1 and 2 of 'Leila's Game'. Use the activity sheet to choose four important events that happen in the first two chapters, and draw a quick picture to describe it.

Underneath each event, explain why you think it is important.

First event

This is important because

Second event

This is important because

Third event

This is important because

Fourth event

This is important because

Learning outcome:

Recognize key events, explaining why they are important to the story.

Writing Composition

Write a report of Leila's first basketball game for the school newspaper. Use the information about the game on pages 28-30 to help you. Look at the words and phrases the author has used to describe the game.

Headline:

Leila's First Game ends in triumph

Article:

Caption:

Learning outcome:

Recall significant events in the form of a newspaper article

STRAND 2 Wayfarers

Title: Timbuktu
Author: Kathryn Harper

Strand 2
Genre: Non-fiction

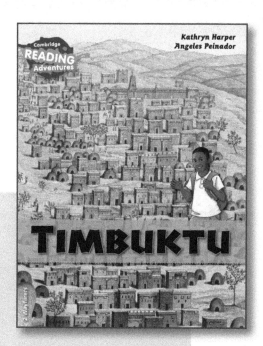

Overview

This book combines history, geography, fact and legend to explore the city of Timbuktu in Mali, Africa. The book uses a narrative voice, as the character of Musa shares his experiences with the reader, as well as a range of other appropriate genre styles. Illustrations are used alongside photographs to compare old and new Timbuktu. A conclusion is drawn about preserving the past for future generations.

Learning outcomes

Children can:

- consider how choice of layout and design relates to the intended audience
- note how sentence structure choices convey the author's intent and meaning
- use phonic/spelling knowledge, along with grammatical and contextual cues, to solve new or unfamiliar words.

Language structure

- Grammatical constructions follow the expected conventions for the genre, including first person narrative: 'I live in a big desert' (p.6), 'I love learning about things' (p.16), and past tense for non-chronological report.
- The voice of the narrator serves to engage the reader: 'Let me tell you all about it' (p.2), 'Look at this piece of salt' (p.8).

Book structure/visual features

- Diagrams, maps and charts exemplify the points made.
- Labels, captions and fact boxes support the information in the main text.

Vocabulary and comprehension

- Topic-specific vocabulary (such as 'ebony' and 'ivory' on p.7) is supported through non-fiction devices in the text or defined in the glossary.
- The narrative voice supports comprehension through establishing a dialogue with the reader (see p.8, for example).

Curriculum links

Geography – Musa tells the reader that Timbuktu is a hard place to reach. Use maps to locate Timbuktu, and use the internet to explore the travel options to that country from your region.

History – Research the real historical figure of Mansa Musa. You may also wish to find out more about the salt trade, linked with other aspects of trade and commerce (such as silks and spices) relevant to your region.

Using the activity sheets

Reading Comprehension: In guided reading, you will have been drawing children's attention to new or unfamiliar words, and getting a sense of their definition from the context. This activity sheet helps to consolidate that work.

Writing Composition: Unusually, this non-fiction book is told using a first-person narrative. Note the features of this style of writing to support the children to write an account of their own region.

Reading Comprehension

Word definition

The author uses many interesting and exciting words to describe Mansa Musa's famous journey from Timbuktu to Mecca.

Look at the words below and think what they might mean. Use the ideas in the text to help you. You can check with a dictionary – but have a go yourself first!

legendary

staffs

exotic

mysterious

Mansa Musa was Emperor of Mali about 700 years ago.

Mansa Musa's caravan was truly **legendary**. In total, about 60,000 people travelled in the caravan. There were families, traders, and servants. They dressed in fantastic clothes in bright and beautiful colours. Even the slaves dressed in silk and carried staffs decorated with gold.

There were lots of animals to help move the people, food and gifts. Each camel carried 150 kilos of gold. At night, the caravan stopped and the tents were set up and meals were prepared. After a long day travelling, people needed a good sleep.

As the caravan passed through towns and villages, people couldn't believe their eyes. The caravan was so long, so rich and so exotic. It seemed never-ending. Every so often, Mansa Musa stopped and gave gold to poor people. They must have been surprised when this great emperor stopped to give them gold!

Soon, people all over the world start talking about this emperor and his amazing caravan. They become very **curious** about his wonderful and mysterious empire in the middle of Africa.

11

Are there any other words you did not know in this passage from 'Timbuktu'? Find out what they mean.

Learning outcome:

Using the context to define new or unfamiliar words

Writing Composition

Find out as much information as you can about where you live, ready to write your own book like 'Timbuktu'. Use books and on-line websites to help you.

Here are some ideas to help you begin your research …

Find a map of where you live. Do you live near a river or the sea? How easy is it for travellers to reach your country?

Find out about a famous historical figure from your region.

What did he or she do that made them famous?

Masu told us about the Djinguereber Mosque of Timbuktu.

Is there a famous building or place where you live that you could tell your reader about?

Learning outcome:

Write in the personal voice to describe real life events and record information.

Title: The Digger
Author: Jim Eldridge

Strand 2
Genre: Fiction

Overview

Dak finds a broken-down digger. He is determined to make it work again. A wide range of characters and events over time add to the complexity of this story. The strong themes address more global issues, such as access to clean water and transportation.

Learning outcomes

Children can:

- consider the impact of grammatical devices in building tension and supporting comprehension

- understand how narrative structure, paragraph and chapter breaks serve to build tension and position the reader

- analyse techniques used by the author to portray character.

Language structure

- Reporting clauses are appropriate to action and character (for example, 'he begged silently' on p.15; 'protested Dak' p.18).

- The order of clauses in sentences conveys the author's intent and supports comprehension, for example in denoting the passing of time ('It was another two weeks before ...' on p.19).

Book structure/visual features

- A strong storyline provides opportunity for readers to consider the cause and effect of a character's actions and motive.

- Paragraphs serve alongside purposeful chapter breaks to clearly signal the development of events.

Vocabulary and comprehension

- Unknown or unfamiliar words are supported by context, sentence structure and spelling pattern.

- Strong characterisation supports children to infer characters' feelings.

Curriculum links

Geography – There are many different dams around the world. Use the Internet and other non-fiction sources to investigate dams, and write a non-chronological report.

Science – Experiments with forces, building small model dams in sinks or tubs of water, would explore how successful different types of materials are in holding back water.

Using the activity sheets

Reading Comprehension: One way the author builds tension is by noting the passing of time. Identify words and phrases that demonstrate that throughout the story.

Writing Composition: Children will have been thinking about how the author portrays characters in the story. The writing activity asks children to respond to questions in the character of Dak.

Reading Comprehension

The author of 'The Digger' uses different phrases to explain to the reader how time is passing in the story. Look through the book and collect some examples of how he does this. Remember to write the page where you found your example. The first one has been done for you.

On page 8
Weeks turned into months …

On page _____

On page _____

On page _____

On page _____

Learning outcome:

Identifying words and phrases that show the passing of time in stories

Writing Composition

Dak's digger saved the village. Dak was very brave.

A reporter from the town went to the village to interview Dak for the newspaper. How do think Dak would answer these questions?

How old are you, Dak?

Have you lived in the village all your life?

Tell me about mending the digger. Did you do it all by yourself?

What happened on the night of the flood?

How did you feel?

What are you going to do now?

Learning outcome:

To write in role as a character from the story

Title: Diving Under The Waves
Author: Andy Belcher

Strand 2
Genre: Non-fiction

Overview

In this non-fiction book, readers can discover how diving has developed from a human desire to see the world underwater to a popular sport and a form of exploration. Historical facts are combined with technical information, such as informing the reader about how divers can breathe underwater. There is an element of persuasion, considering the importance of conservation to preserve marine habitats, which is an appropriate level of challenge for Strand 2 readers.

Learning outcomes

Children can:

- identify non-fiction text features, using these to aid comprehension

- summarise the main ideas from one or more paragraphs, using these to explain their understanding to others

- read complex sentences accurately, paying attention to punctuation and querying when the meaning is unclear.

Language structure

- Conventions for non-chronological report are followed, for example in the use of present tense: 'good lighting is essential' (p.24) and generic subjects, such as 'divers' and 'scientists'.

- Sentences are longer and more complex, including embedded phrases ('In cold regions, like the Arctic, divers cut holes ...' on p.23) requiring careful reading for comprehension.

Book structure/visual features

- A logical structure is employed to take the reader through the development of diving methods from early free-diving to the techniques of the present day.

- The book incorporates a range of text features, appropriate to the subject matter, including fact boxes to describe true-life historical events, and diagrams, such as to show how a pearl is formed (on p.7).

Vocabulary and comprehension

- Accurate technical vocabulary is used ('snorkel', 'salvage', 'buoyancy'), with the meaning supported by the context and by an extensive glossary.

- Emotive vocabulary, such as 'fragile', 'protect', 'responsibility', 'be careful', is used on pp.28-29 to persuade the reader of the need for conservation.

Curriculum links

Science – There are many scientific experiments related to water and the sea. For example, children could explore salt water density: take two same size water jugs. Fill both with water. To one, add a large amount of salt. Now explore what happens when objects are lowered into the different jugs of water (eggs work particularly well for this experiment).

Art – Using the wonderful description of the marine worlds underwater, create a collage of a coral reef, including the different sorts of creatures that live there. Children may want to add a few divers and a shipwreck, too.

Using the activity sheets

Reading Comprehension: Use the activity sheet to support the learning objective to summarize the key ideas in a paragraph. You will have demonstrated this during the guided reading lesson.

Writing Composition: Using the information provided in the text, and from other non-fiction sources, children write as a diver exploring an underwater shipwreck for the first time.

Reading Comprehension

GOING SCUBA DIVING

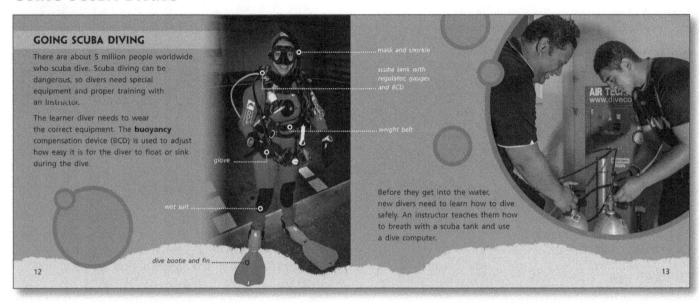

Turn to pages 12 and 13 of 'Diving Under the Waves'.

There are three paragraphs on this spread. Use the boxes below to identify the main ideas in each paragraph.

The key idea in the first paragraph is:

The key idea in the second paragraph is:

The key idea in the third paragraph is:

Learning outcome:

Summarize the main ideas from one or more paragraphs

Writing Composition

EXPLORING SHIPWRECKS

Pages 20 to 22 of 'Diving Under the Waves' explain what it is like to explore underwater shipwrecks.

Imagine you are a diver. Describe what you might see and feel diving to see a wreck. Use the information in the book to help you.

Name _____ Date _____

Exploring the Shipwreck

It was the dive of a lifetime: the first time anyone had seen the ship since it

sank over 200 years ago.

_____

_____

_____

_____

_____

_____

_____

_____

_____

_____

Learning outcome:

Use information from non-fiction sources to write a fiction account

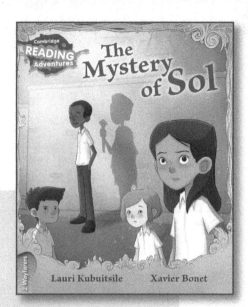

Title: The Mystery of Sol
Author: Lauri Kubuitsile

Strand 2
Genre: Play

Overview

This play is written to be read aloud in guided reading lessons. It features six characters so that each member of the group can have a speaking part. The play follows the style of a mystery story as Ava and her friend Cherie try and discover the truth about Sol. Inferential reading is supported, as the two girls discover clues to the identity of their mysterious new class mate.

Learning outcomes

Children can:

- identify key features of playscripts, using directions to aid expression when reading
- compare the recording conventions of speech in plays with that written in narrative
- evaluate the way their reading sounds when reading aloud, considering how well emotions are portrayed.

Language structure

- Dialogue is punctuated appropriately to aid reading with meaning and expression.
- Sentences lengths vary. Characters often speak in short sentences (e.g. *'Kill him? But why?'* on p.19) with the narrator speaking longer, more explanatory ones (as on p.24).

Book structure/visual features

- Playscript conventions are followed, including a cast list and stage directions.
- Acts and scenes delineate the passing of time and sequence of events.

Vocabulary and comprehension

- Stage directions (*'whispering'* p.2; *'sadly'*, p.15) support reading aloud with expression.
- Scenes end with a question or cliff hanger to create suspense.

Curriculum links

PSHE – The rules in Ava and Cherie's school seem very different to the ones Sol and Lonny are familiar with. The story could be a basis for an examination of rules in school and how they are designed for the safety and well-being of children.

Literacy – Whilst this mystery is written as play, children could explore other mystery stories, looking at the features of the genre.

Using the activity sheets

Reading Comprehension: In guided reading, you will be asking the children to consider character intent and motive. The activity sheet considers a dilemma for the two girls in the story.

Writing Composition: Children can follow up their reading by producing a short video of the story. They can produce storyboards to capture important events and characterisation in each scene.

Reading Comprehension

In 'The Mystery of Sol' (page 18) Lonny asked Ava not to tell anyone. But do you think Ava and Cherie should tell their teacher? Give reasons for your answer.

Learning outcome:

Consider character intent and motive, and how this affects the outcome of the story.

STRAND 2 Wayfarers

Writing Composition

Storyboard – Act 2 Scene 2 (pages 18-20)

In this scene, Lonny explains to Ava why he and Sol are hiding. Imagine that you were making a video of this scene. Draw sketches and write what each character would be speaking and feeling.

Learning outcome:

Pick out key events in a scene, mapping how the scene would look and how the characters respond to the situation.

STRAND 2 Wayfarers

Title: You and Me
Author: Lynne Rickards

Strand 2
Genre: Poetry

Overview

'You and Me' is a poetry anthology focused on family and friendship. The poems in this book reflect a range of experiences across ages and cultures, providing opportunity to compare and contrast ways in which the themes are explored.

Learning outcomes

Children can:

- identify different patterns of rhyme and verse in poetry
- explore poetry writing conventions, considering the effect across the different poems
- compare and contrast poems on similar themes, considering preferences and giving rationales.

Language structure

- A range of poetic styles is used, appropriate to subject and setting.
- Sentence structures are varied in order to convey feelings, and to support reading aloud with rhythm and prosody.

Book structure/visual features

- Different structural features are used, such as varying line length, rhyming patterns and layout on the page.
- Illustrations support the main theme of each individual poem within the anthology.

Vocabulary and comprehension

- Opportunity to explore rhyme and syllabification, and consider effect in oral reading.
- Use of imagery and poetic, figurative language to convey meaning.

Curriculum links

PSHE – Use this book in studies about how people live: families, friendship, people who help us.

Literacy – Children can explore other poetry anthologies, considering different ways in which these are compiled (for example, poems for specific age groups, or around certain topics). Children could compile their own anthologies, with favourite poems to make up the collection.

Using the activity sheets

Reading Comprehension: This poetry anthology contains poems on the theme of family and friendship. You will be asking children to discuss their preferences in the guided reading lesson, and can use the activity sheet to follow-up this discussion.

Writing Composition: The activity sheet asks the children to begin to plan a poem to write. Writing poetry is not easy. Once children have thought of an idea for their poem, work together in guided writing to support them.

Reading Comprehension

My favourite poem in 'You and Me'

This is a book of poems all about family and friendship. What is your favourite poem? Write about why you have chosen this poem.

My favourite poem is

I like it because

Does your poem rhyme?

Would you recommend this poem to a friend?

Why?/Why not?

Who or what would you write a poem about, and why?

Learning outcome:

To evaluate poetry and to discuss preferences

Writing Composition

'You and Me' - Planning a poem

The poems in 'You and Me' are all about families and friends. Who would you like to write a poem about?

My poem is about ....

I have chosen this person to write about because ....

....

....

....

Look at how the poet in 'You and Me' has a different subject for each verse (look at 'Home Time' on p.14, for example). What will be the subject of each of your verses?

Verse 1	Verse 2

Verse 3	Verse 4

Add extra verses if you need to.

Now you have planned your poem. Work with your teacher to begin to write it.

Learning outcome:

To plan a poem, based on the framework of a poem read

STRAND 2 Wayfarers

Title: Who is the Greatest?
Author: Anita Ganeri

Strand 2
Genre: Non-fiction

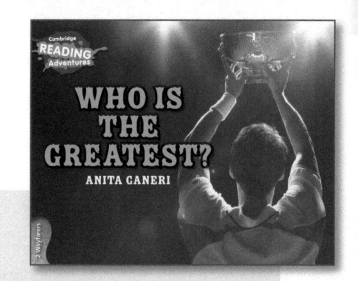

Overview

Young sports lovers will enjoy this book which draws together some of the greatest sportsmen and women of all time, and poses the reader a challenging question: which one is the greatest of all? The book explores each sportsperson's life and achievements, supported by high quality photography and a host of fascinating facts, making this an interesting non-fiction read.

Learning outcomes

Children can:

- consider the impact of adverbs and adverbial phrases, noticing authorial intent to position the reader

- distinguish between fact and opinion in reading

- analyse how texts can be organised differently, suggesting reasons for these differences.

Language structure

- Elements of biography and journalistic writing are employed.

- Sentences are more becoming complex, but with clear structural support and effective punctuation choices to aid comprehension.

Book structure/visual features

- A set format and layout is employed to explore the life and achievements of each sportsperson featured.

- The author sets a purpose for reading, in seeking to establish who is the greatest sportsperson ever, and returns to this question in the concluding part of the book.

Vocabulary and comprehension

- Appropriate technical vocabulary is used, specific to each of the sports represented, such as 'Grand Slam' (p.4), 'slam dunk' (p.16), 'pole position' (p.19).

- Expressive language ('power and dedication to training', p.4; 'he scored an incredible 326 runs' p.12) is used to build mood and to position the reader.

Curriculum links

History – This book covers a range of different sports. Children may wish to focus on one particular sport such as football or cricket, and research the 'greatest' in each chosen field.

Maths – Greatness in sport is often judged by measurement – highest, fastest, longest, strongest. Chart and measure the children's results as they try out different athletic activities in the school gym or playground.

Using the activity sheets

Reading Comprehension: Following discussion about the use of adjectives and adjectival phrases in the guided reading lesson, children can complete the activity sheet to note their use and consider their effectiveness.

Writing Composition: Children use the activity sheet to research a famous sportsperson of their own choosing. Demonstrate how they will complete this, by referring to the text layout and paragraph contents in 'Who is the Greatest?'

Reading Comprehension

Usain Bolt

Read page 6 from 'Who is the Greatest?'. The author has used lots of adjectives and adjectival phrases to describe Usain Bolt and his life. Can you find some examples? The first one has been done for you.

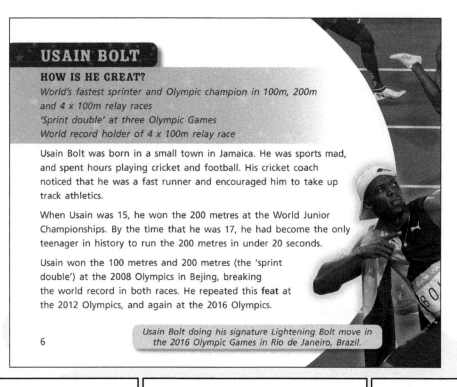

★ USAIN BOLT

HOW IS HE GREAT?
World's fastest sprinter and Olympic champion in 100m, 200m and 4 x 100m relay races
'Sprint double' at three Olympic Games
World record holder of 4 x 100m relay race

Usain Bolt was born in a small town in Jamaica. He was sports mad, and spent hours playing cricket and football. His cricket coach noticed that he was a fast runner and encouraged him to take up track athletics.

When Usain was 15, he won the 200 metres at the World Junior Championships. By the time that he was 17, he had become the only teenager in history to run the 200 metres in under 20 seconds.

Usain won the 100 metres and 200 metres (the 'sprint double') at the 2008 Olympics in Bejing, breaking the world record in both races. He repeated this **feat** at the 2012 Olympics, and again at the 2016 Olympics.

6

Usain Bolt doing his signature Lightening Bolt move in the 2016 Olympic Games in Rio de Janeiro, Brazil.

a small town in Jamaica		

Do you think Usain Bolt is the greatest? Explain why or why not.

_____

_____

_____

What other words or phrases would you use to describe Usain Bolt?

_____

_____

_____

Learning outcome:

To identify adjectives and adjectival phrases and to consider the impact these create for the reader.

Writing Composition

My Greatest Sportsperson

Name _____

HOW IS S/HE GREAT?

_____

_____

_____

_____

_____

_____

_____

FACT FILE

_____

_____

_____

_____

_____

_____

Learning outcome:

Use the layout of a non-fiction text to write their own biography of a famous sportsperson.

STRAND 3 Explorers

Title: A Tale of Two Sinbads
Author: Ian Whybrow

Strand 3
Genre: Fiction

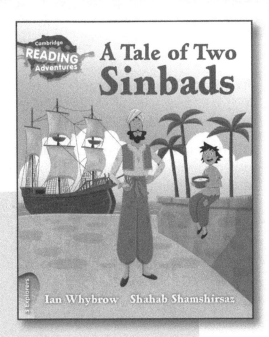

Overview

The third story of Sinbad in the Cambridge Reading Adventures finds our hero returning home after a long and eventful voyage at sea. The story is told in three distinct parts as Sinbad regales his adventures to a young boy, also known as Sinbad. Themes of kindness and bravery enable young readers to explore actions and consequence.

Learning outcomes

Children can:

- recognise authorial devices used to position the reader: through layout, chapter breaks and vocabulary choice
- consider the effectiveness of language structures and expressions used
- analyse features of legends, identifying techniques of retelling in this style.

Language structure

- Traditional retelling devices are used, for example: *'The boy listened quietly as the story began.'* (p.11).
- Characters are described through gesture or non-verbal comment, for example, *'there was a twinkle in his eye'* (p.26).

Grammar and sentence structure

- Opportunity to explore different forms of story structure through the retelling.
- Illustrations serve to visualize characters and settings, whilst requiring readers to infer and interpret information.

Vocabulary and comprehension

- Vocabulary choices infer character traits (e.g. *'horrified'* p.15) to describe how Sinbad was feeling, rather than these being overtly stated.
- Opportunity to infer from character actions, for example, considering why Sinbad kept his identity hidden.

Curriculum links

Literacy – The legends of Sinbad have been retold in many different ways. Children could collect and explore a variety of retellings.

Geography – Sinbad sails the Seven Seas. The story could form part of a study on sea travel, plotting the journeys he took.

Using the activity sheets

Reading Comprehension: In the second guided reading lesson, you will be prompting children to look for clues in the text that indicate how the story will end. Draw children's attention to these as you return to text at the end of lesson two.

Writing Composition: Demonstrate to the children how to use the story mountain to make notes and plan a new adventure for Sinbad.

Reading Comprehension

How will it end?

At the end of Chapter Four, Sinbad the Sailor finished telling his adventures to the boy Sinbad. How do you think the author will finish the story in Chapter Five? What clues are there in the text that make you think that?

I think Sinbad the Sailor might ...

I think this because ...

Or perhaps the boy Sinbad will ...

I think this because ...

Or maybe ...

I think this because ...

Learning outcome:

Use the clues provided by the author to predict the outcome of the story.

Writing Composition

Sinbad's Mountain Adventure

Sinbad the Sailor is off on another adventure. This time his journey takes him over a mountain. Sinbad usually meets some fantastic creatures on his journeys. What will he meet in your story? Start at the bottom of the mountain and climb up to plan Sinbad's new adventure.

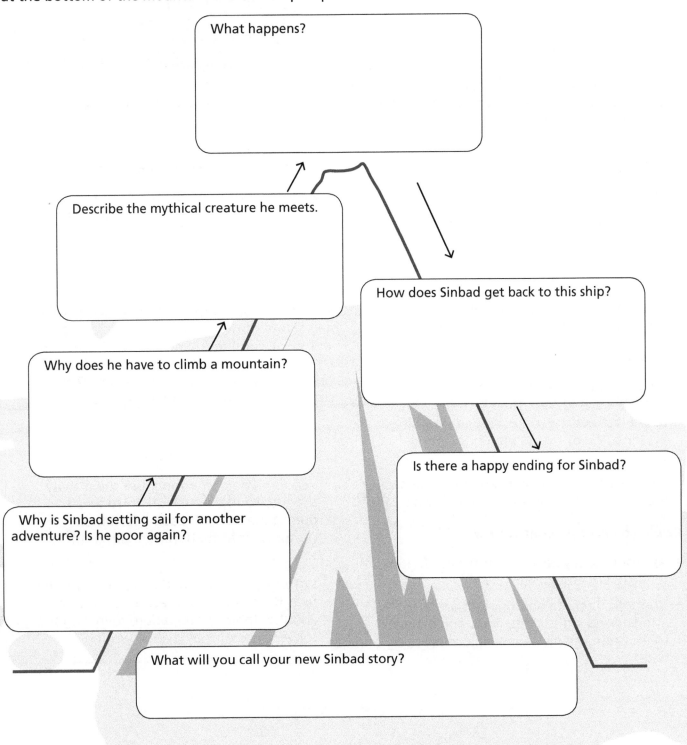

What happens?

Describe the mythical creature he meets.

How does Sinbad get back to this ship?

Why does he have to climb a mountain?

Is there a happy ending for Sinbad?

Why is Sinbad setting sail for another adventure? Is he poor again?

What will you call your new Sinbad story?

Learning outcome:

To use known features of traditional tales to create a new adventure story.

STRAND 3 Explorers

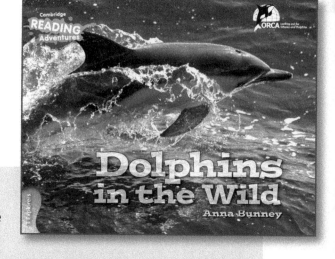

Title: Dolphins in the Wild
Author: Anna Bunney

Strand 3
Genre: Non-fiction

Overview

Features of non-chronological report and persuasive writing, with some elements of instruction, are used in this mixed-genre non-fiction text to explore how dolphins live in the wild, before considering efforts to conserve this endangered species for future generations.

Learning outcomes

Children can:

- use a range of non-chronological report sources to gather information
- record and present information on a given topic
- consider authorial intent, seeking evidence in the text to support their conclusion.

Language structure

- Appropriate voice and register is used: generic voice for reporting sections with direct instructions to the reader regarding preservation of the dolphin population.
- Grammatical choices, such as the use of adverbial words and phrases ('*Unfortunately*', '*However*') demonstrate the author's position.

Book structure/visual features

- Appropriate layout and non-fiction design features are employed.
- Dramatic, real-life photographs are interspersed with tables, maps and diagrams to illustrate the messages explored in the main text.

Vocabulary and comprehension

- Subject-specific vocabulary is used appropriately, supported by additional information in facts boxes and a comprehensive glossary.

Curriculum links

Art and Design – Explore and evaluate design and layout of non-fiction texts (including websites), considering how well information is relayed. For example, are there additional features that do not support the facts? Would a chart have aided the reader's understanding?

Using the activity sheets

Reading Comprehension: Use the activity sheet to support the work introduced during the guided reading lesson on capturing information from different sources.

Writing Composition: Children can use the facts they found to create a newsletter about dolphin conservation, following the conventions of that style of writing.

Reading Comprehension

Key Facts About Dolphins

Fact 1		
Fact 2		
Fact 3		
Fact 4		
Fact 5		

Learning outcome:

Use a range of information sources to compare facts about dolphins.

Writing Composition

Date:

SAVE THE DOLPHINS

By:

Tell your reader what your article is going to include.

In this issue:

Did you know … ?

Get your reader's attention! Why should they read your article?

Discuss what is being done to help dolphins survive in the wild.

Preserving the dolphins

Fact Box

State three important facts to explain why dolphins are endangered.

Add a picture and a caption.

Learning outcome:

To record information about a subject from texts read.

STRAND 3 Explorers

Title: Journey to Callisto
Author: Mauritz DeRidder

Strand 3
Genre: Mixed genre

Overview

Written in a non-fiction style, this book is set sometime in the future and explores the potential for a space mission to Callisto to establish a space colony. Using the voices of the mission commander and the crew members, the book uses a variety of non-fiction features and fiction genre to explore the possibility and logistics of such a journey – could it ever come true?

Learning outcomes

Children can:

- consider how vocabulary and grammar choices influence the reader's comprehension and engagement with the text
- evaluate the effective use of a range of text types
- visualise events and characters from the information provided in the text.

Language structure

- Written in the appropriate voice, such as reporting in the impersonal voice: *'Jupiter has over sixty moons …'* (p.12) and first-person narrative: *'I have dreamt of this moment all my life'* (p. 27).
- Language structures convey a futuristic or scientific sense: (*'Once in orbit around Jupiter …'* (p.33); *'Transfer food and oxygen supplies'* (p.34) to help set the scene for the reader.
- Grammatical structures are used accurately to aid reader engagement, for example imperative verbs in the procedural section on p.34, and the use of persuasive language features: *'the most exciting and historic event in history'*, *'greatest adventure of your life'* on pp.38-39.

Book structure/visual features

- A mix of photographs, illustrations and diagrams maintain the non-fiction feel of the book; although the book is telling an imagined event, it is based on scientific fact.

Vocabulary and comprehension

- Vocabulary choices (*'zero gravity'*, *'colony'*, *'asteroid belt'*) serve to demonstrate the space setting and context.
- The role of the different narrators supports the understanding of the different complex tasks each undertake.

Curriculum links

PSHE – Consider the crew members who travelled on board the Callisto Voyager. If it were possible to take another crew member, what sort of person would you send to establish a new colony and why? What qualities would be needed?

Science – Use 'Journey to Callisto' as part of a study on space and space travel to explore the possibility of flight to distant moons and planets.

Using the activity sheets

Reading Comprehension: Children will be using the information in the text to consider if Captain Yasmin will be a good captain. Look at how she makes quick decisions and how she will look after the crew. She also demonstrates she is brave.

Writing Composition: Use page 39 to talk with the children about whether they would like to join to crew on the voyage to Callisto. Discuss the skills and qualities crew members would need and how they would face up to the dangers. Complete the activity sheet 'Job Application'.

Reading Comprehension

CAPTAIN YASMIN

Captain Yasmin has a very important job to do. Do you think she will be a good captain? Read the text of 'Journey to Callisto', and find places where the author gives us a clue.

Here is an example:

On page 14, Captain Yasmin tells the other crew members that she thinks Callisto is a good place to go.

On page _____,

On page _____,

On page _____,

I think Captain Yasmin will be a good captain because . . .

Learning outcome:

Imagine events and characters from the information provided in the text.

Writing Composition

Can you see yourself as a future colonist? Are you young, fit and healthy? Do you think you could make the 2 year voyage and become a useful member of the colony on arrival? If you do, then come and join the Callisto Colony Project.

Job Application

Your name

Age

Address

Please answer the following questions:

What was your previous job? Why do you want to leave it?

Why do you want to join the crew of the Callisto Voyager?

What special skills or qualities do you think you bring to the job?

How do you feel about the risk involved in undertaking such a journey?

Learning outcome:

Use information from the text to write in a different style or genre.

STRAND 3 Explorers

Title: Skyscrapers
Author: Chris Oxlade

Strand 3
Genre: Non-fiction

Overview

In this non-fiction text, children find out all sorts of amazing facts about the building and design of skyscrapers. Using a mix of report and explanatory features, the book looks at the historical development of skyscrapers through to the tallest towers of the present day.

Learning outcomes

Children can:

- consider how choice of layout and design relates to the intended audience
- summarise the main ideas from one or more paragraphs
- explore less familiar words and phrases in context to ascertain meaning.

Language structure

- Sentences adhere to the expected conventions for the genre (e.g. explanation sections written in past tense with chronological signposting: 'first', 'then', 'now', p.20).
- Complex sentences are supported by strong structures to aid comprehension.

Book structure/visual features

- Logical progression through from the historical development of skyscrapers and how they were built, to present day techniques and challenges.
- Photographs are interspersed with diagrams and drawings to support the text content.

Vocabulary and comprehension

- Subject-specific vocabulary (such as 'ducts' and 'cables' on p.14) is introduced and defined within the text or included in the glossary.
- Text features combine to support comprehension of more complex aspects, as in the mix of diagram, fact box, labels and text on p.14, to describe skyscraper services.

Curriculum links

Design Technology – Children could experiment with pulleys to design and build their own miniature lifts.

Maths – Children could work on charting these buildings from the shortest to the tallest, arranging them in scale, adding other tall buildings, including those in their own region, to the chart.

Using the activity sheets

Reading Comprehension: In the first guided reading lesson, the children will have read to page 15. You will have asked them to identify some key facts and new information about skyscrapers. The activity sheet asks children to record these facts and where they found them.

Writing Composition: By summarising the main events in paragraphs, children begin to learn how to take notes from texts read to inform their own writing.

Reading Comprehension

IMPORTANT FACTS ABOUT SKYSCRAPERS

You have read up to page 15 in your guided reading lesson. You will have found out some new and important things about skyscrapers.

Write the three most important facts you found out. Be ready to discuss these with your group in your next guided reading lesson.

On page _____, I found that

On page _____, I found that

On page _____, I found that

Learning outcome:

To identify new and important facts from the texts read.

Writing Composition

HOW SKYSCRAPERS ARE BUILT

Pages 20 to 23 describe how a skyscraper is built. Write one or two lines that summarise the main idea in each of the paragraphs on these pages.

Page 20

First paragraph

_____

_____

_____

Second paragraph

_____

_____

Page 21

_____

_____

Page 22

_____

_____

Page 23

_____

_____

Now you can use your summary to write your own description of how a skyscraper is built.

Learning outcome:

To summarize the main idea of a paragraph

Title: The Changing Climate
Author: Jon Hughes

Strand 3
Genre: Non-fiction

Overview

This book explores the facts and opinions surrounding climate change: an important topic around the world. Going back to prehistoric times, the book tracks the changing climates the world has experienced, and discusses the potential impacts of global warming on the world today.

Learning outcomes

Children can:

- locate relevant information in the text and present this is in an appropriate form for a given audience

- express personal responses to text, such as considering the usefulness and clarity of certain features

- consider whether statements are fact or opinion, and identify evidence in the text which supports their decision.

Language structure

- Sentences are of greater complexity, and include multiple clauses: *'scientists need to look at what happened in the past to help understand clues about what might happen in the future'* (p.4).

- Appropriate technical vocabulary and language structure is used for the message being given and received, such as in the question and answer dialogue between members of the public and the scientists on pp.22 and 23.

Book structure/visual features

- A range of appropriate non-fiction features is employed, including diagrams to explain more complex scientific concepts.

- A mix of chronological and non-chronological reporting is used to explain the historical perspective and the current position of climate change.

Vocabulary and comprehension

- The language of causality (*'This happens because the water in the seas and oceans is changing temperature and affecting the temperature on the land.'* p.19) and of persuasion (*'people need to plan and adapt if they are to survive in a changing climate'*, p.29) is used to position the reader and convey the author's message.

- Diagrams, captions and labels support the main text, adding further information to support the reader's comprehension.

Curriculum links

Science – There are many different science investigations related to global warming. For example, children could collect data to chart the temperature of different countries across a period of time, using information from the internet to compare with the average temperature for the time of year.

Humanities – Children could investigate places around the world which are affected by the impact of climate change, such as flooding in Bangladesh or drought in parts of the Africa. Look at how people in these lands are finding ways to adapt to the changing conditions.

Using the activity sheets

Reading Comprehension: Encourage the children to express their opinions about this text, and to evaluate its success in providing clear and accessible information.

Writing Composition: Children will use the pictograms created in guided lesson three to pull together facts about global warming, looking at differing opinions and drawing conclusions.

Reading Comprehension

A CHANGING CLIMATE – A BOOK REVIEW

Briefly, explain what this book is about:

_____

_____

_____

Look at pages 4 and 5. Did you find the diagram useful? Explain why/why not.

_____

! What was the most interesting thing you learned?

_____

_____

Overall, what do you think of this book?

I thought that

I rate this book: ☆ ☆ ☆ ☆ ☆ (colour how many stars)

because _____

Learning outcome:

To express personal opinions about a non-fiction text

Writing Composition

The planet is getting hotter!

Use your pictograms from the guided reading lesson to write a discussion about global warming.
Here are some sentence starters to help you.

Millions of years ago . . .

Today . . .

Scientists think . . .

However, some other people think . . .

If the climate continues to warm, then . . .

I think that . . .

In the future, energy could be made by . . .

Learning outcome:

Use information from the text in a different form for a chosen audience and purpose.

Title: Hunters of the Sea
Author: Tony Bradman

Strand 3
Genre: Fiction

Overview

This book follows the adventures of a young boy kidnapped and forced to work on a whaling ship. Written in five chapters, the story deals with sophisticated and complex themes, matched to the young reader's growing maturity.

Learning outcomes

Children can:

- interpret indicators of character through dialogue and action

- consider the use of vocabulary and language structure to convey meaning

- view events from the perspective of each of the different characters.

Language structure

- Speech patterns and structures, such as 'You will only speak when you're spoken to, boy!' (p.10) demonstrate character and motive.

- Sentences have greater complexity, with multiple clauses.

Book structure/visual features

- A strong plot and complex structure is supported by paragraphing and chapter organisation.

- Illustrations help to visualize the characters and settings whilst allowing for the reader's interpretation of events.

Vocabulary and comprehension

- Specific vocabulary choices serve to convey meaning and intent, as in the use of powerful verbs in reporting clauses, and to support the story setting and context: 'Ahoy down below! There she blows ...' (p.14).

Curriculum links

Natural History – Whales are an endangered species. Use the story as a basis for investigations into conservation of the whale population. See, also 'Giants of the Ocean' (Gold Band) and 'Dolphins in the Wild' (Strand 3) in Cambridge Reading Adventures.

Using the activity sheets

Reading Comprehension: At the end of the first guided reading lesson, you will have reached the 'cliff-hanger' at the end of Chapter Three. Discuss with the children how to use the activity sheet to record effective word choices and sentence structures on p.18 of this chapter.

Writing Composition: Demonstrate how to identify words and phrases that the author uses to describe characters in the story. Use these to write a character study of a chosen character.

Reading Comprehension

THE KILLING OF THE WHALES

In Chapter Three, the boy experiences the full horrors of whaling for the first time as *The Nimrod* chases and kills three Sperm Whales. Then the whales' bodies are brought on board.

Read the passage below and underline some words and sentences that describe the terrible scenes the boy witnesses. Write why you think they are effective. There is an example already done for you.

Then came the worst part. The bodies were tied to the *Nimrod*, and we towed them to a nearby island. There, they were dragged on to the beach and the crew set to work cutting them up. Within a few hours, the men had filled a great number of barrels with meat and oil, leaving just the enormous skeletons of those beautiful creatures.

It was the saddest thing I had ever seen. I could feel tears rolling down my cheeks as my stomach churned with the awful stench. Sam explained that whales were worth lots of money, but only when they were dead. People liked eating whale meat, and they used the oil in lamps. In fact, almost every part of a whale was useful in one way or another. But hearing that didn't make me feel any better.

This is a powerful verb which describes how the boy felt.

'Ah, so you don't like the way we make our living,' said Captain Coffin, scowling at me. 'Well, I can see I'm going to have to help you learn to love it.'

His words chilled me to the bone.

Learning outcome:

To consider how word choice and sentence structure help to convey sense and meaning in the text.

Writing Composition

A CHARACTER STUDY

Choose a character from the story. Find words and phrases the author uses to help describe your character.

How my character looks ...		How my character acts ...

My character is

_____

How other characters respond to my character ...		How my character talks ...

Now write a short description of your character

_____

_____

_____

Learning outcome:

To identify how character is portrayed through speech and action.

Title: Movie World
Author: Colin Millar and Spike Breakwell

Strand 4
Genre: Non-fiction

Overview

An extensive coverage of aspects of film and movie-making, this non-fiction book explores the historical development of the film industry through to the present day, and explains how a film is made. A mixed genre approach is adopted, including historical report and biography.

Learning outcomes

Children can:

- recognise different non-fiction text types, exploring why a writer might choose to write in a particular genre for audience and purpose

- skim and scan text effectively to support fast research and recall

- identify features of biography, using them in their own writing.

Language structure

- Appropriate grammatical devices are used to support the different text purposes, as in the use of fronted adverbials to denote the passing of time ('*Four years later ...*', '*only 16 years after ...*', p.5).

- Words and phrases, specific to the movie industry are employed, such as '*Lights, camera, action!*' on p.3.

Book structure/visual features

- The various genre styles are clearly identified across different sections of the book, for example, in the historical reporting of early movie-making (pp.4-5).

- Photographs with appropriate captions support the main text.

Vocabulary and comprehension

- Topic-specific vocabulary (such as '*editing*' and '*trailer*' on p.37) is supported through non-fiction devices in the text or defined in the glossary.

- The author's vocabulary choices position the reader: '*He was so good ...*' (p.20); '*outstanding animations ... wonderfully imaginative stories*' (p.13).

Curriculum links

Science – Explore a range of scientific experiments related to photography and film, such as creating pinhole cameras and designing flick-book animations.

Literacy – Using the example of a film review on pp.38-39, children can write reviews of their favourite film, or of one that they didn't enjoy, giving personal reasons and seeking to persuade the reader.

Using the activity sheets

Reading Comprehension: In the guided reading lesson, you will have demonstrated and supported children to locate and recall facts by skimming and scanning the text. The activity sheet helps to reinforce those skills.

Writing Composition: Throughout the book there are several short biographies of film celebrities. Use these as an example of how children can research and write their own biographies of their favourite stars.

Reading Comprehension

THE EARLY DAYS OF FILM

Use the index, glossary and facts boxes to find answers to the following questions. Record the page where you found this information.

What was the first movie film ever recorded? Who made the film and where?

I found my answer on page _____

What were the 'Talkies'?

I found my answer on page _____

Which animated film first featured Mickey Mouse?

I found my answer on page _____

Describe what is special about the Anime style of animation.

I found my answer on page _____

Now write a question of your own for a friend to answer:

Learning outcome:

To skim and scan a non-fiction text to retrieve information

Writing Composition

PLANNING A BIOGRAPHY

In 'Movie World', you read a biography of Charlie Chaplin (page 6). Chaplin was a famous film star in the early days of film-making.

Who is your favourite film star? Use books and the Internet to find out all about them. Use the information you find to write a biography.

Name of my film star

Early life

How they became famous

Most famous films

Interesting facts about my film star

Why I chose this person ...

Learning outcome:

Use the features of biography to write about a favorite film star.

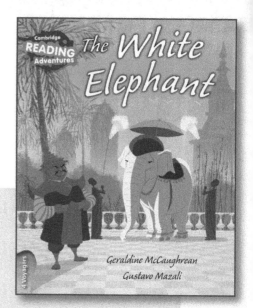

Title: The White Elephant
Author: Geraldine McCaughrean

Strand: 4
Genre: Fiction

Overview

In this story, Preecha is handed a White Elephant as a punishment, but his good sense and honesty lead to a positive outcome. This book is written in the style of a traditional story, incorporating many of those features. Events occur over time, illustrating the changing fortunes and intentions of the main characters. The story itself plays on the notion of a 'White Elephant' as a possession or gift that is difficult or expensive to maintain.

Learning outcomes

Children can:

- use the key points of a story to summarise events over time

- identify authorial techniques which use grammatical structures to position the reader

- evaluate word choice, for example in the use of figurative or emotive language.

Language structure

- Literary phrases are used to enhance the traditional style, such in as the repetition of 'Tell me, for I am very stupid'.

- Implied events to come, for example: 'The new moon rose like the curved dagger the king wore at his wide, wide waist.' (p.16).

Book structure/visual features

- Chapter headings delineate both the passing of time ('Next Morning'; 'Nearly Two Years Later') and significant shifts in events ('Dead') to engage the reader.

Vocabulary and comprehension

- Vocabulary choices portray the use of irony. For example, on p.6, the king is not really rewarding Preecha, but punishing him for speaking his mind.

- Effective verb choice supports characterisation, for example in helping the reader identify with the king's true intention (p33).

Curriculum links

Natural History – Elephants are an endangered species under threat from hunting and poaching for their ivory tusks. Children could investigate true life examples of conservation projects set up to preserve and protect elephants living in the wild.

Using the activity sheets

Reading Comprehension: You could use the activity sheet to support your teaching in lesson 3. Children can complete the activity, following the lesson.

Writing Composition: At the end of guided reading lesson two, you will have discussed with the children the potential outcomes of Preecha's decision to release Rosy the elephant into the wild. Use the activity sheet to help the children think about the impact these outcomes would have on the story. (Please note - Rosy being killed is not an option! The story needs to continue ...).

Reading Comprehension

Events Over Time

The story of 'The White Elephant' takes place over a sequence of time: Preecha has to keep and look after the elephant for two years (page 6).

Look through the book and find key words and phrases that indicate what happens over those two years. Plot the events on the timeline below.

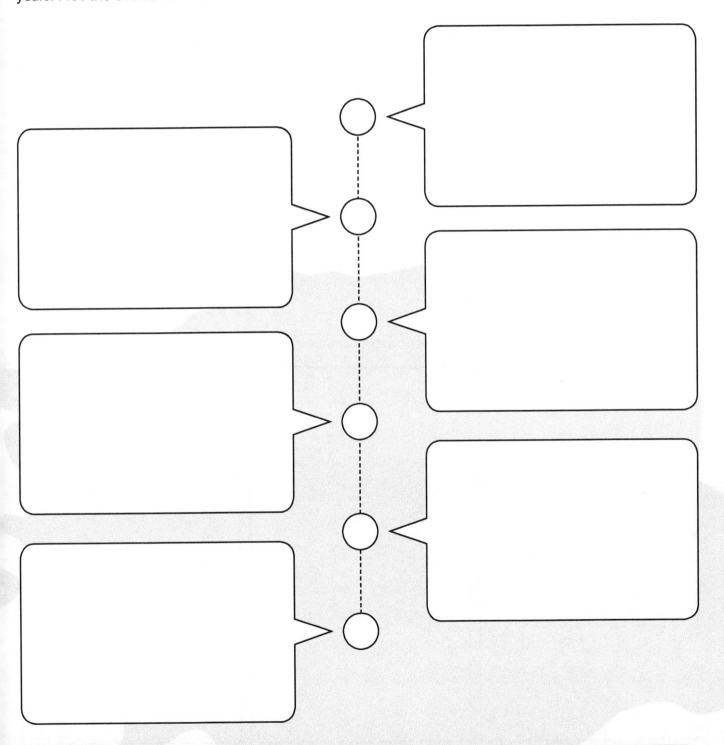

Learning outcome:

To identify key events in the story to summarize events over time.

Writing Composition

In 'The White Elephant', Preecha decides to let Rosy the elephant free to live in the wild. His family are very worried about this.

Why do you think they are worried? Think about three possible things that might happen to Rosy, and how that outcome might affect how the story continues.

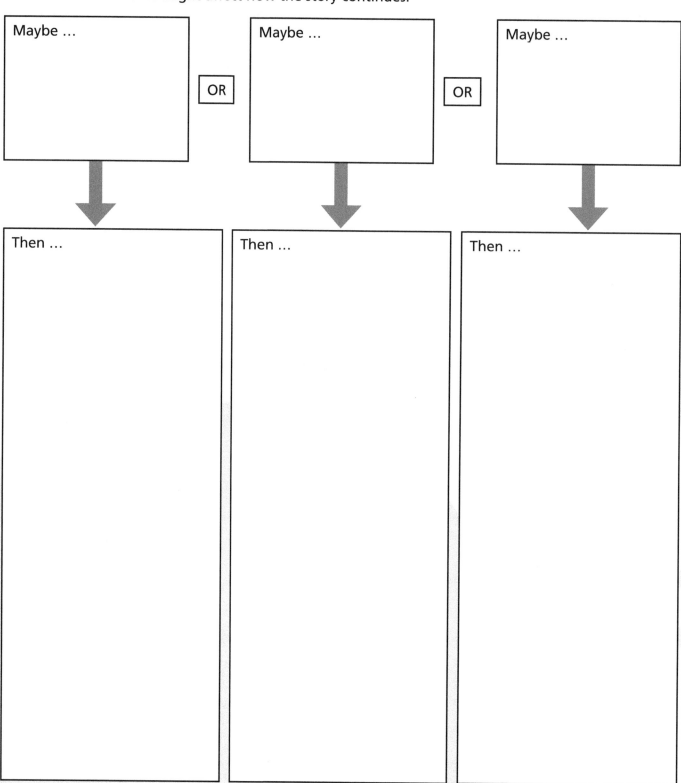

Maybe …

OR

Maybe …

OR

Maybe …

Then …

Then …

Then …

Learning outcome:

To predict possible outcomes, based on key events in the story so far.

STRAND 4 Voyagers

Title: Meltdown
Author: Peter Millet

Strand 4
Genre: Fiction

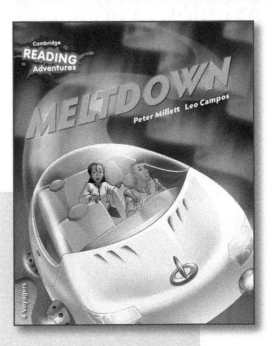

Overview

This science fiction story is set sometime in the future. Mahira and her brother try and find their way home in a city without power after a solar flare hits the Earth and causes an electrical meltdown. In the conclusion, Mahira ponders the lessons learned from the event. The futuristic setting provides opportunity for children to bring their prior knowledge and experience to a novel context.

Learning outcomes

Children can:

- recognise narrative structure techniques (such as flashbacks) and consider their effectiveness
- understand how genre forms can be used in different contexts
- identify authorial intent through use of grammatical structures and conventions.

Language structure

- Technical language and structure is used to maintain the setting: '*Our planet was bombarded with so much solar energy and radiation*' on p.5.
- Imagery (such as '*the chilling roar of roaming lions*', on p.11) and simile ('*we must have glowed like a tinfoil ball*' on p.5) are used to support the reader to interpret actions and motivations.

Book structure/visual features

- Chapter headings add to the futuristic nature, written as date and time to indicate the writing in a journal.
- Events are not linear: the main character, Mahira, recalls past events and looks to the future, whilst writing in the present.

Vocabulary and comprehension

- Authentic use of words in context (e.g. '*travel pods*', '*megacity*', '*holograms*') to support the science-fiction genre.
- Appropriate vocabulary choices aid characterisation, for example '*annoyed*' '*snappy*', (on p.25) to show the children are becoming stressed.

Curriculum links

Science – Children could survey the range of electrical appliances they use, and consider alternative sources of energy.

History – Examine items that have been superseded by digital technology, for example, in the recording of sound.

Using the activity sheets

Reading Comprehension: In the second guided reading lesson, you will have discussed with the group how the author creates suspense and give insights into character through certain vocabulary choices and grammatical structures. Use the activity sheet to follow up this lesson.

Writing Composition: 'Meltdown' is written as a journal. Discuss in guided reading the features of such writing. The activity sheet gives children opportunity to use this style of writing to explore another of the characters in the story.

Reading Comprehension

WHAT SHALL WE DO?

Read to page 25 of 'Meltdown' On this page, Samir and Mahira argue about what they should do next.

Think about their different points of view. Note the words and phrases the author uses to give you a clue about their feelings.

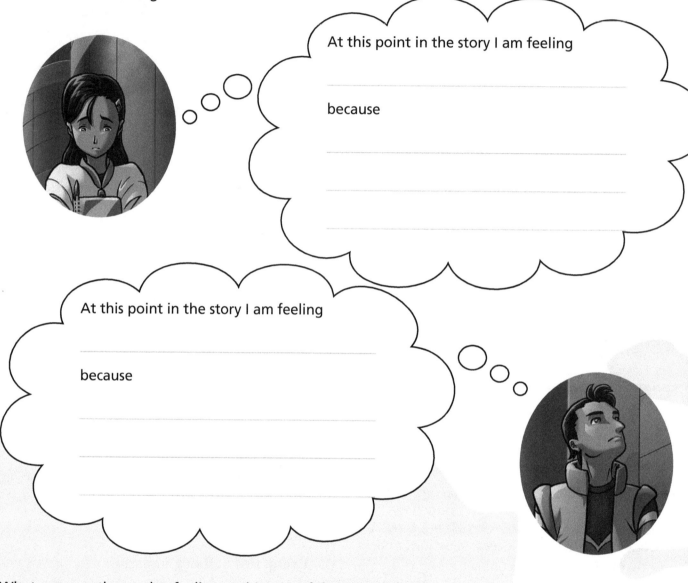

At this point in the story I am feeling

_____

because

_____

_____

_____

At this point in the story I am feeling

_____

because

_____

_____

_____

What are you, the reader, feeling at this part of the story? Why?

_____

_____

_____

_____

Learning outcome:

How character action and intent is portrayed through authorial word choice

Writing Composition

WRITING A JOURNAL

'Meltdown' is written in the form of a journal. Mahira records the events and her personal thoughts as the disaster is happening

How would Samir record the same events In his journal? Think about things that happened to him during the story, and how he sometimes disagreed with Mahira's decisions.

Write Samir's journal account for the events of 24-10-2148 (pages 8-13).

REMEMBER:

- Write in the first person, using 'I', as if you were Samir.
- Make sure Samir tells his reader what he is thinking and feeling.

24-10-2148

You could also write Mum's journal for the same day. What might she be doing whilst Mahira and Samir are looking for her?

Learning outcome:

Explore the techniques of journal/diary writing, using flashbacks and accurate grammatical structures.

Title: The Cave at the End of the World
Author: Chris Powling

Strand: 4
Genre: Fiction

Overview

The story of Tig and her brother, Uga, is set in prehistoric times. Through Tig's desire to be an artist, the story explores the origin of Stone Age cave paintings, and suggests how they came to be hidden for thousands of years. Sustained over seven chapters, and with multiple events over time, the book provokes emotional engagement and response from the reader, and provides opportunity for sustained reading.

Learning outcomes

Children can:

- identify how character is built up as events occur, considering the impact on motives and action

- use what they know of narrative structure to summarise the story's key events and recognise how grammatical structures are used to convey meaning and position the reader.

Language structure

- A stylistic feature in this book is how the characters reveal their inner thoughts to the reader, as on p.13, where Tig encourages herself to keep going.

- Sentences vary in length, and different punctuation techniques (such as in the use of questioning on p.15) help to create effect.

- Adverbial phrases and complex sentences support the narrative structure.

Book structure/visual features

- Chapter headings effectively outline the key events in the story.

Vocabulary and comprehension

- Powerful vocabulary is used to describe characters, such as the first introduction to the old man on p.7.

- More complex sentences make pronoun resolution more challenging: *'Before long, they could smell the thin, sour smoke of it'* (p.18), requiring inferential reading.

Curriculum links

History – Research the discovery of actual cave paintings, using the Internet.

Art – Experiment drawing in the style of cave paintings, paying attention to the choice of colour (natural pigments) and appropriate subject matter (animals and hunting scenes).

Using the activity sheets

Reading Comprehension: The activity sheet follows the guided reading lesson, investigating how the author's choices in sentence construction can influence the meaning and emphasis.

Writing Composition: Children can use what they know of the characters, and previous experience of reading playscripts (for example, 'The Mystery of Sol' at Strand 2) to turn a section of narrative into a playscript for reading aloud.

Reading Comprehension

Read this passage from page 19 of 'The Cave at the End of the World'.

> For a moment, lit by the slow-burning torch, the old man and the young man stared angrily at each other, then Tig tugged at the old man's sleeve. 'You can trust him,' she said. 'He was just protecting me the way he always does. He'll keep your den secret, I promise.'
>
> 'You think so?"
>
> "I know, he will,' said Tig, firmly.

Look at the first part of the opening sentence:

**'For a moment, lit by the slow-burning torch, the old man
and the young man stared angrily at each other'.**

Why has the author chosen to write in this particular order?

Explore placing the parts in a different order. Which would be most powerful, do you think? Do you agree with the author?

stared	for a moment	lit by the slow-burning torch

angrily	the old man and the young man	at each other

Now look at the dialogue at the end of the passage:

'You think so?"

'I know, he will,' said Tig, firmly.

1 Who is speaking in the first line?

_____

2 Why do you think the author did not tell us?

_____

_____

3 What do you notice about these two sentences? Think about why they are different to the other sentences in the passage.

_____

_____

4 Think about the author's use of the word 'firmly'. What does this tell us about Tig at this point in the story?

_____

Learning outcome:

To consider how word choice and sentence structure influences meaning and emphasis

Writing Composition

REWRITING A SCENE AS A PLAYSCRIPT

Look at page 26. This is the first time Tig sees inside the magnificent cave full of paintings. She is going to paint a woolly mammoth.

There is little dialogue on page 26, so you will have to turn the characters' thoughts into words for the play.

When you are planning, you will need to think about:

words and phrases which describe how the three characters are thinking and feeling:

Tig	Uga	The Old Man

Think about how to start. Who would speak first? Would you need to give a stage direction? Use other playscripts you have read to help you set out your play.

Learning outcome:

Write as a playscript to consider how character is portrayed as events occur.

Title: The Refugee Camp
Author: Jim Eldridge

Strand: 4
Genre: Fiction

Overview

Ahmed's dream is to play professionally for a European football team – it is his hope for a better life for himself and his family. This story of triumph over adversity offers opportunity to explore different points of view. The challenging themes emerging (bullying, effects of war) have capacity for emotional engagement and in-depth reaction.

Learning outcomes

Children can:

- explain their views to others and listen to points of view which may differ from their own
- recognise narrative structure techniques (such as flashbacks) and consider their effectiveness
- identify ways in which grammatical conventions and language structures support reading comprehension.

Language structure

- Emotive language ('*I hate my life here*' p.16) describes character feeling.
- Grammatical conventions support the action and character responses, such as short sentences for impact.

Book structure/visual features

- Events occur over time and in flashback.
- Chapters support the build-up and suspense of the narrative.

Vocabulary and comprehension

- Word choices challenge comprehension, such as in the use of adverbs to support characterisation ('*determinedly*' on p.21) and specialist language ('*penalty*', '*deflected*', '*striker*' on p.24).
- The writer evokes a response in the reader, for example when Bozan breaks down in tears (p.15).

Curriculum links

Geography – Children could investigate their favourite teams, mapping the countries of origin of the players.

PSHE – Use Ahmed's experiences and real-life news items to explore sensitively the plight of refugee children in different parts of the world.

Using the activity sheets

Reading Comprehension: Chapter 3 of 'The Refugee Camp' details Bozan's change of heart. Look for the evidence of this with the children. Demonstrate how to use this information to complete the comprehension activity sheet.

Writing Composition: In the third guided reading lesson, you will have read the exciting football match, drawing attention to how the author engages the reader's interest. Remind the children what they know of how newspaper articles are written. They can use this prior knowledge to rewrite the match as a report for the camp newsletter.

Reading Comprehension

BEFORE AND AFTER

The character of Bozan is an important one in 'The Refugee Camp'. Think about how he changes as the story develops. Look for places in the text that tell us how and why he changes.

How is Bozan feeling at the start of the story?

BEFORE

CAUSE

How does Bozan feel at the end of the story?

AFTER

How does Bozan behave at the start of the story?

How does Bozan behave at the end of the story?

What happened to make Bozan change?

Learning outcome:

To chart character development as events unfold in the story, and to consider reasons for changes seen.

Writing Composition

WHAT A MATCH!

Chapter Four of 'The Refugee Camp' tells about the football match between the International All-Stars and the camp team. The author uses many interesting words and phrases to make it sound an exciting match!

Use the pages in this chapter to write a report of the match for the camp newspaper.

Remember to use the techniques a reporter would use:

• Powerful words and sentences;

• Interviews with the players at half-term and after the match;

• Not using 'I' or 'you' as you are reporting the events as they happened.

Name your newspaper

Write your headline

Add a picture	Describe the first half

And a caption

Describe what happens to Bozan. What would he say to the reporter?	Describe how Ahmed saves the day. What would he say to the reporter?

Learning outcome:

Use grammatical and structural features of articles to rewrite the match for a newspaper report.

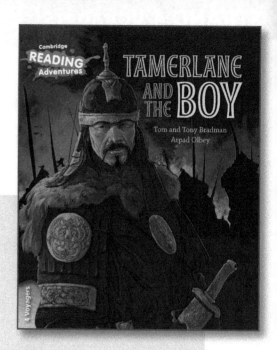

Title: Tamerlane and the Boy
Author: Tom and Tony Bradman

Strand: 4
Genre: Fiction

Overview

This story is based on historical fact. Tamerlane was a great and fearsome warrior who conquered and massacred many people in regions such as Russia, Afghanistan and India. This retelling focuses on an event in Georgia, where Tamerlane showed some mercy in the face of the bravery of one young boy. Using authentic, historical retelling techniques, the story explores sensitive themes of loss, cruelty and hardship.

Learning outcomes

Children can:

- explain how they have been affected by what they have read, referring to text to support their responses

- identify how character motives and actions change as result of events

- comment on word choice which influences how the reader interprets authorial intent.

Language structure

- Simile is used for effect, such as 'like ... a lamb to the slaughter' on p.32.

- Sentences are longer and require complex pronoun resolution (see p.18, for example).

Book structure/visual features

- Story plot involves a series of chronological events of cause and effect, building to a resolution.

- Chapter breaks support identification of key developments in the story, and build tension.

Vocabulary and comprehension

- Authentic and appropriate vocabulary choices ('scabbard', 'fine silk tunic') help set the historical context.

- Effects are created through descriptive language: 'a tangle of charred roof timbers and rubble' on p.24, for example.

Curriculum links

History – Tamerlane is a true historical figure from the 1400s. He is known by several different names including Temur, Amir Timur and Tamburlaine. Children can use the Internet to research the historical figure and compare with the portrayal in 'Tamerlane and the Boy'.

Using the activity sheets

Reading Comprehension: In the first guided reading lesson, you will have explored how the author creates mood and effect though vocabulary choices. The activity sheet will reinforce what children have learned in this lesson.

Writing Composition: Prompt the children to recall what they know of non-fiction historical recount. Ask them to rewrite the story of Tamerlane and the Boy as if it was a real event, using the writing frame to help.

Reading Comprehension

WORDS AND MOODS

Reread Chapter 2 of 'Tamerlane and the Boy'. Look for ways in which the author has created the mood through his choice of words and phrases. Think about the way these affect you as the reader.

On page _____, the author used the word:

_____

This was a good word to use because:

_____

_____

On page _____, the author wrote:

_____

_____

_____

I felt _____, because

_____

On page _____, the author used the word:

_____

This was a good word to use because:

_____

_____

On page _____, the author wrote:

_____

_____

I felt _____, because

_____

_____

On page _____, the author used the word:

_____

This was a good word to use because:

_____

_____

On page _____, the author wrote:

_____

_____

I felt _____, because

_____

Learning outcome:

Note and comment on how author word choices can influence the reader

Writing Composition

TAMERLANE – THE RULE OF TERROR

Although Tamerlane is a real historical figure, the story of his meeting with Kioni is fiction. Now you have finished reading the story, rewrite the events as if they really happened.

Look at some non-fiction history books to help you.

REMEMBER:

- Write in the past tense;
- Report the facts as if they happened;
- In a historical recount you do not address the reader directly (using 'you') or write about yourself (using 'I').

Paragraph 1 Write some background information about Tamerlane (see page 6 to help you).

Paragraph 2 Describe the events when Tamerlane's men came to Kioni's village.

Paragraph 3 Retell the meeting of Kioni and Tamerlane in the camp.

Paragraph 4 Write the conclusion to Kioni's adventure.

Learning outcome:

To rewrite the story in a different genre, following the conventions for that style of writing.

Mapping and Correlation Chart (Strands 1 to 4)

Band	Title	Fiction/ non-fiction	Author	Cambridge Assessment International Education Primary English Curriculum Framework Links	International Primary Curriculum links	IB Primary Years Program topic links	Cambridge Global English Unit Links
STRAND 1: Pathfinders	Four Clever Brothers	F	Lynne Rickards	Read playscripts and dialogue, with awareness of different voices; Read and perform playscripts, exploring how scenes are built up; Begin to infer meanings beyond the literal, e.g. about motives and character.	Milepost 1 Unit: The Stories People Tell	Who we are	Grade 5 - Unit 6: Myths and Fables
STRAND 1: Pathfinders	Honey and Toto: the story of a cheetah family	NF	Jonathan and Angela Scott	Read and evaluate non-fiction texts for purpose, style, clarity and organisation.	Milepost 3 Unit: What a Wonderful World; the Natural World	How the world works	Grade 5 - Unit 9: Planet Earth
STRAND 1: Pathfinders	River Rescue	F	Peter Millett	Use knowledge of punctuation and grammar to read with fluency, understanding and expression.	Milepost 3 Unit: Go with the Flow; Weather and Climate	How the world works	Grade 3 - Unit 5: Inventors and Inventions
STRAND 1: Pathfinders	Connections	NF	Scoular Anderson	Read and evaluate non-fiction texts for purpose, style, clarity and organisation.	Milepost 2 Unit: Invention that Changed the World; Milepost 3 Unit: Making New Materials; The Time Tunnel	Where we are in place and time	Grade 6 - Unit 5: Inventions
STRAND 1: Pathfinders	The Mountain of Fire	F	Peter Millett	Understand how expressive and descriptive language creates mood.	Milepost 2 Unit: Active Planet; Milepost 3 Unit: What a Wonderful World	How the world works; Who we are	Grade 4 - Unit 5: Getting Around
STRAND 1: Pathfinders	Leila's Game	F	Spike Breakwell Colin Millar	Use knowledge of punctuation and grammar to read with fluency, understanding and expression; Investigate how settings and characters are built up from details and identify key words and phrases.	Milepost 3 Unit: Express Yourself - Feelings	Who we are	Grade 4 - Unit 1: Family Circles

Mapping and Correlation Chart

Band	Title	Fiction/non-fiction	Author	Cambridge Assessment International Education Primary English Curriculum Framework Links	International Primary Curriculum links	IB Primary Years Program topic links	Cambridge Global English Unit Links
STRAND 2: Wayfarers	Timbuktu	NF	Kathryn Harper	Identify unfamiliar words, explore definitions and use new words in context.	Milepost 3 Unit: Building a Village: Settlements; History - AD 900: History of Non-European Societies	Where we are in place and time	Grade 5 - Unit 7: Ancient Civilisations
STRAND 2: Wayfarers	The Digger	F	Jim Eldridge	Read widely and explore the features of different fiction genres; Learn how dialogue is set out and punctuated.	Milepost 2 Unit: Living Together - Community	Who we are; Sharing the planet	Grade 5 - Unit 8: Weather and Climate
STRAND 2: Wayfarers	Diving Under The Waves	NF	Andy Belcher	Skim read to gain an overall sense of a text and scan for specific information; Look for information in non-fiction texts to build on what is already known.	Milepost 3 Unit: What a Wonderful World; Milepost 3 Unit: Science - Water for Everyone	How the world works	Grade 6 - Unit 3: Sport
STRAND 2: Wayfarers	The Mystery of Sol	F	Lauri Kubuitsile	Read and perform playscripts, exploring how scenes are built up; Begin to infer meanings beyond the literal, e.g. about motives and character; Consider how choice of words can heighten meaning.	Milepost 2 Unit: Different Places, Similar Lives: Similarities and Differences	Who we are	Grade 4 - Unit 2: Stories
STRAND 2: Wayfarers	You and Me	F	Lynne Rickards	Compare and contrast poems and investigate poetic features.	Milepost 2 Unit: Living Together - Community; Milepost 3 Unit: Express Yourself - Feelings	Who we are; How we express ourselves	Grade 5 - Unit 1: Talking about People
STRAND 2: Wayfarers	Who is the Greatest?	NF	Anita Ganeri	Skim read to gain an overall sense of a text and scan for specific information; Read and evaluate non-fiction texts for purpose, style, clarity and organisation.	Milepost 2 Unit: They made a Difference; Milepost 3 Unit: Fit for Life	Who we are	Grade 6 - Unit 3: Sport Grade 5 - Unit 5: Famous People

Band	Title	Fiction/ non-fiction	Author	Cambridge Assessment International Education Primary English Curriculum Framework Links	International Primary Curriculum links	IB Primary Years Program topic links	Cambridge Global English Unit Links
STRAND 3: Explorers	A Tale of Two Sinbads	F	Ian Whybrow	Read and identify characteristics of myths, legends and fables; Learn how dialogue is set out and punctuated.	Milepost 2 Unit: Explorers and Adventurers - Discovering the World; Milepost 3 Unit: Myths and Legend	Who we are; Where we are in place and time	Grade 5 - Unit 5: Famous People
STRAND 3: Explorers	Dolphins in the Wild	NF	Anna Bunney	Skim read to gain an overall sense of a text and scan for specific information; Read and evaluate non-fiction texts for purpose, style, clarity and organisation.	Milepost 3 Unit: What a Wonderful World	How the world works	Grade 5 - Unit 9: Planet Earth
STRAND 3: Explorers	Journey to Callisto	NF	Mauritz deRidder	Identify unfamiliar words, explore definitions and use new words in context; Extract key points and group and link ideas.	Milepost 3 Unit: Space Explorers	Where we are in place and time; How the world works; How we organize ourselves	Grade 6 - Unit 6: Explorers
STRAND 3: Explorers	Skyscrapers	NF	Chris Oxlade	Skim read to gain an overall sense of a text and scan for specific information.	Milepost 2 Unit: Inventions that Changed the World - How Things Work; Milepost 3 Unit: Buiding a Village - Settlements?	How the world works	Grade 5 - Unit 3: Where we Live
STRAND 3: Explorers	The Changing Climate	NF	Jon Hughes	Read and evaluate non-fiction texts for purpose, style, clarity and organisation; Extract key points and group and link ideas.	Milepost 3 Unit: Climate Control	How the world works; Sharing the planet	Grade 5 - Unit 3: Where we Live
STRAND 3: Explorers	Hunters of the Sea	F	Tony Bradman	Comment on a writer's use of language and explain reasons for the writer's choices; Comment on a writer's use of language, demonstrating awareness of its impact on the reader.	Milepost 3 Unit: What a Wonderful World	Who we are; How the world works	Grade 5 - Unit 9: Planet Earth

Band	Title	Fiction/non-fiction	Author	Cambridge Assessment International Education Primary English Curriculum Framework Links	International Primary Curriculum links	IB Primary Years Program topic links	Cambridge Global English Unit Links
STRAND 4: Voyagers	Movie World	NF	Spike Breakwell Colin Millar	Skim read to gain an overall sense of a text and scan for specific information; Read and evaluate non-fiction texts for purpose, style, clarity and organisation; Compare the language, style and impact of a range of non-fiction writing.	Milepost 2 Unit: Inventions That Changed the World	Where we are in place and time; How we express ourselves	Grade 6 - Unit 4: The Big Screen
STRAND 4: Voyagers	The White Elephant	F	Geraldine McCaughrean	Begin to interpret imagery and techniques, e.g. metaphor, personification, simile, adding to understanding beyond the literal; Explore proverbs, sayings and figurative expressions.	Milepost 3 Unit: What a Wonderful World	How the world works; Who we are	Grade 5 - Unit 9: Planet Earth
STRAND 4: Voyagers	Meltdown	F	Peter Millett	Understand aspects of narrative structure, e.g. the handling of time; Understand language conventions and grammatical features of different types of text.	Milepost 3 Unit: Science - Full Power! Electricity; What Price Progress? Invention and Development	Who we are; Where we are in place and time; How the world works; How we organize ourselves	Grade 5 - Unit 3: Where we Live
STRAND 4: Voyagers	The Cave at the End of the World	F	Chris Powling	Look for implicit meanings, and make plausible inferences from more than one point in the text;Understand changes over time in words and expressions and their use.	Milepost 3 Unit: They see the World like this: Artists Impressions of the World	Where we are; How we express ourselves	Grade 6 - Unit 1: Life Experience
STRAND 4: Voyagers	The Refugee Camp	F	Jim Eldridge	Comment on a writer's use of language, demonstrating awareness of its impact on the reader; Discuss and express preferences in terms of language, style and themes.	Milepost 3 Unit: Express Yourself - Feelings; Moving People - Migration; Here and Now, There and Then - Host Country and Home Country	Sharing the planet; Who we are; Where we are in place and time	Grade 6 - Unit 3: Sport
STRAND 4: Voyagers	Tamerlane and the Boy	F	Tom and Tony Bradman	Analyse the success of writing in evoking particular moods, e.g. suspense; Explore use of active and passive verbs within a sentence.	Milepost 3 Unit: History - AD900: History of Non-European Societies	Who we are; Where we are in place and time	Grade 5 - Unit 6: Myths and Fables

STRAND 1
Pathfinders

STRAND 2
Wayfarers

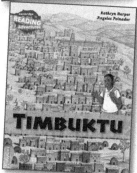

STRAND 3
Explorers

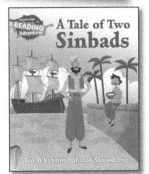

STRAND 4
Voyagers

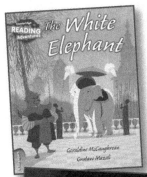

SECTION 3: READING ASSESSMENT

Reading Assessment

Successful guided reading relies on the teacher's careful selection of books, matched accurately to the children's current reading attainment. At the Early and Transitional stages of Cambridge Reading Adventures, teachers will be using a running record to ensure that the texts are at just the right instructional level. A running record is designed predominantly to capture early reading behaviour at word and sentence level, in order that teachers can look more closely at what sources of information children are using or neglecting.

At the Conventional stage, reading will be almost entirely accurate, and the teaching and learning focus turns towards comprehension. Therefore, teacher assessment will focus on whether the child is maintaining a sense of meaning of the story, reading beyond the literal text and making inferences, or reading for information effectively in non-fiction books.

To ascertain whether a child is ready to move onto the next strand, teachers carry out a review of current reading competency and comprehension. An assessment can also alert teachers to areas of development within the strand.

Please note: we do not advise completing an assessment after each book.

Guided reading lessons provide ample opportunity for 'on the run' assessment of progress. More formal assessment procedures are only required when teachers need to make informed decisions about whether to move a child to another strand, or to focus teaching on a particular area of comprehension.

Carrying out the reading assessment.

Unlike the early stages, there is no prescribed benchmark text at the Conventional stage. Teachers can select any unseen book from within the child's current strand.

Follow the procedure outlined below.

Summarising task

Provide the child with adequate time to read the book quietly and independently. Prepare the child for the task, saying: *'After you have finished reading, I will talk to you about the book and you can tell me about what you were reading'.*

When the child has finished reading, ask them to summarise the story (if reading fiction) or identify the main points of the text (if reading non-fiction). Record their responses. Note, for example, if the child retold the story confidently. Did they add any extra information or personal commentary? Did they use pictures or refer to the text to support the retelling? Were events recalled in sequence?

Please note: if the child is unable to give a succinct and relevant summary, this may indicate that the child should be reading at an earlier strand, or band.

Reading accuracy and fluency

Choose two or three pages for the child to read aloud to you. It may not necessarily be the beginning of the book. It could be a key chapter or a focus of interest in a particular topic. Do not prompt or support during the reading. Whilst the child is reading, note down any miscues or errors they make, for example how the child approached reading an unfamiliar multisyllabic word. Listen to how the reading sounds (reading fluency) recording, for example, attention to punctuation and text layout to aid expression. Note whether the reading sounded phrased or whether the text was read too fast, or in a staccato manner. Was intonation used appropriately? See the completed examples (pages 128–131) for guidance on how to record.

Please note: if there are multiple errors (more than 1 in 10) in the reading, the text is too hard and comprehension will be affected. It may indicate that the child should be reading at earlier strand, or from banded texts.

If you have concerns about the retelling and the reading accuracy, **DO NOT** proceed with the comprehension part of the assessment. The text will be too hard for the child to access the meaning successfully. This child needs further support to develop reading skills. Take a running record of the text to obtain a more diagnostic picture of the child's reading behaviours (see the Cambridge Reading Adventures Early and

Transitional Teacher Guides for information on how to administer a running record assessment).

Questions to assess understanding

This assessment builds on the three comprehension skills introduced in earlier stages of Cambridge Reading Adventures: recalling, inferring and responding. At the Conventional stage there are five comprehension skills addressed:

- **Recalling** – the answers are literal and drawn specifically from the text. Answers need to be accurate.

- **Understanding vocabulary** – the child demonstrates ability to access word meaning from the text and from their own understanding

- **Inferring** – these questions require children to read 'between the lines' of the information in order to draw conclusions and gain meaning – the answers are not explicitly stated in the text.

- **Responding** – children are asked questions which 'go beyond the text' to explain, evaluate and comment on the content. There will often be multiple, reasonable responses to responding questions, with no one right answer. Teachers will make a judgement based on the plausibility of the answer and their knowledge of the child.

- **Relating to different contexts** – acknowledging social and emotional aspects of the text. Questions ask children to explore the significance of what is written to their own context or previous reading, bringing personal views and experience to consideration of character motive and plot development.

Comprehension assessment questions framework

A set of questions for each book is provided (see pages 116-118 of this Teaching and Assessment Guide). These provide a structured progression of one of each question type across the four strands. In addition, teachers can add further diagnostic questions based on outcomes from the guided lesson, relevant to their own children and context.

Completing the assessment

Summarise the comprehension assessment, noting information about how the child answered the questions, for example by referring back to the text or looking at illustrations. Think about what type of questions the child found the most challenging.

Recommendations
This section enables the teacher to review the observations and consider next steps for this child. The teacher will then need to look at the text characteristics for the next strand (see p. 22-29 in this Teaching and Assessment Guide) and decide, on the basis of the evidence collected, whether the child is ready to progress.

Two completed exemplar assessments are included for guidance, one fiction and one non-fiction.

Reading Assessment

Comprehension Assessment Questions – Strand 1

	Four Clever Brothers	Honey and Toto: the story of a cheetah family	River Rescue	Connections	The Mountain of Fire	Leila's Game
Recalling	Why did Gilead think the four brothers had stolen his camel?	Why was the cub called 'Toto'?	Why did Kamon and his father decide not call the police to help the boys?	What was discovered that meant computers could be made even smaller?	Why did the climbers need to abandon the summit climb?	Who won the game of backgammon?
Understanding vocabulary	On page 18, what does the word 'judgement' mean?	Can you explain what the authors mean when they say this is 'a story of the triumph of courage' on page 3?	What is a flash flood? Use the information on pages 4-6 to help you describe it.	Describe the binary system. How does it work in a computer?	Agus says to the children 'Your life is in my hands' (p.5). What do you think he means?	In your own words, describe what a 'strategy' is (p.14).
Inferring	What do you think of the character of Gilead? Give reasons for your answer.	Why do lions not want cheetah cubs to grow up (p.22)?	What would have happened if the drone's battery had run out?	Why was life easier when humans stopped moving around (p.8)?	Jun wanted to be the first to reach the top of the mountain. Why?	How did Leila's friends feel about her plan to help them win?
Responding	Do you think Gilead was right to take the brothers to the judge? Explain why you think that.	'Toto was a clever cub' (page 12). Explain some of the things he did that were clever, and why.	Would you say Kamon was brave? Give reasons for your answer.	What do you think gave the first humans the idea that they could make weapons from sharpened stone?	On p.5, why were Rafi and Daniel reluctant to follow Jun? What do you think was worrying them?	What other suggestions do you have that might help the team to play better?
Relating to different contexts	Is the story of the Four Clever Brothers like any other stories you have heard or read? What is similar about them?	We don't know what happened to Toto. How did you feel when you read that he had disappeared?	If you were Kamon, how would you be feeling at the end of the story?	p.26 shows many different types of computers. Which of these inventions do you think is most important in today's world?	Can you think of another title for this story?	Describe the relationship between Leila and her grandfather.

Comprehension Assessment Questions – Strand 2

	Timbuktu	The Digger	Diving Under the Waves	The Mystery of Sol	You and Me	Who is the Greatest?
Recalling	What was salt used for in ancient Timbuktu?	Explain how the digger came to be left in the village.	Name two different types of diving explored in this book.	Explain why Ava thinks 'there's something funny going on' (p.8).	Name two of the amazing things Mr Bing can do (p.12).	What sport is Saïd Aouita famous for?
Understanding vocabulary	What is a 'caravan' in this book? Describe it.	What did Uncle Riv mean when he said: 'You have a good attitude, Dak' on p. 5?	Explain what is meant by 'free-diving'.	What would happen in an Etiquette class (p.5)?	Why is the poem on p. 22 called 'Imagine'?	What does 'faultless' mean on p.24? What helped you work out the meaning?
Inferring	Why were the people surprised when Mansa Musa gave them gold (p.11)?	On p. 15, why were the villagers 'whispering among themselves and smiling knowingly'?	Why do you think new divers need to complete two dives before they can qualify (p.14)?	Explain in your own words how Lonny confused what he overheard (see pages 27-29).	How do you know the boy in the poem doesn't like his new shoes?	Explain why Michael Jordan was such a great basketball player.
Responding	What happened to Timbuktu's Golden Age? Why did it change?	Why do you think the village elder tried to discourage Dak from working on the digger (p.4)?	Explain why divers might dive to a wreck.	Ava says she wants to be a detective. Do you think she would be a good one?	Choose your favourite poem and explain why you like it.	Do you think Michael Phelps was right not to retire before the 2016 Olympics?
Relating to different contexts	Look at the non-fiction features on pages 10 and 11. Explain why these are helpful to the reader.	Dak felt very nervous (p.12). How do you think you would feel? Explain why.	How do you think you would feel if you were a diver in a shark cage (see p. 17)?	Lonny doesn't tell Ava and Cherie the truth about Sol (p.14). Do you think he was right not to?	Did any of the poems remind you of something that has happened to you?	Who would you say is the greatest sportsperson? Give reasons for your answer.

Reading Assessment

Comprehension Assessment Questions – Strand 3

	A Tale of Two Sinbads	Dolphins in the Wild	Journey to Callisto	Skyscrapers	The Changing Climate	Hunters of the Sea
Recalling	How Sinbad know the islanders were really pirates (p.17)?	Explain how dolphins are camouflaged to protect against predators.	Why won't the Voyager be launched from Earth (p.17)?	Who invented the first lift with a safety system?	Using the diagram on p.27, describe how wind power works.	The boy in the story has three names. What are they?
Understanding vocabulary	Why did Sinbad have a 'twinkle in his eye' (p.11)? What does this expression mean?	What do pectoral fins help the dolphin to do (p.5)?	Find a new word you didn't know before and explain what it means.	Why do you think the Flatiron Building (p.7) was so-called?	'The Earth is a very dynamic planet' (p.5). Describe what you think 'dynamic' means.	On p.6, what do you think 'scrawny' means?
Inferring	How did making a fire help Sinbad and his sailors (p.19)?	Why is the presence of dolphins in the sea a sign of a healthy environment?	Crew members were only allowed to take one or two personal items on board (p.31). Why?	Explain why there were no skyscrapers in towns and cities before the 1880s.	Why could humans not have survived on the Earth millions of years ago?	What does Amos mean when he says 'you'll be food for the fishes' on p.8?
Responding	Why do you think Sinbad didn't want to tell the boy his name at first (p.9)?	Why might dolphins fight amongst themselves when swimming in big pods (p.8)?	Five days from the landing (p.34), how do you think the crew members would be feeling?	Do you think there are too many skyscrapers in the world? Give a reason for your answer.	Look at p.23. Do you agree or disagree with the scientist's answer? Explain why.	What evidence can you find that explains the boy's character in the story?
Relating to different contexts	What features of the Sinbad story do you recognise from other traditional tales you have read?	The author says: 'Putting whales and dolphins in tanks for entertainment is wrong' (p.26). Do you agree?	Would you like to go on a space journey to another planet? Explain why/why not.	Think of a good reason for living in a skyscraper today.	Imagine living in a city on water. What would it be like?	On p.26, Captain Coffin was angry when the boy saved the baby Orca. Do you think he was right to be angry?

Comprehension Assessment Questions – Strand 4

	Movie World	The White Elephant	Meltdown	The Cave at the End of the World	The Refugee Camp	Tamerlane and the Boy
Recalling	When was the first animated film produced? What was it called?	Why did the children name the elephant 'Rosy'?	Where were Samir and Mahira when the superflare struck?	How would you describe the Wildness?	What team did Ahmed play for?	How did the boy recognise Tamerlane when he first saw him?
Understanding vocabulary	Use the information in the book (p.37) to explain what the word 'editing' means.	Preecha is a courtier. What do you think a courtier is?	Find some words in the story which indicate that it is set in the future.	Find verbs which describe the old man's character and appearance.	Find words and phrases in the book to describe the life of a refugee.	The author wrote 'Kioni's blood froze in his veins' on p.12. What do you think he means by this?
Inferring	'really big stars demand big wages!' (p.32). Why do you think they can do this?	Explain why the Royal Flower Arranger said 'You poor thing' to Preecha (p.6).	Why were people injured (p.10)? What had happened to them?	Why did the old man come looking especially for Tig?	Why was Bozan crying (p.15)?	On p.14, why did Kioni tell his mother and sister to 'go quietly'?
Responding	'really great movies will be remembered for a long time' (p.42). What would you say makes a great movie?	Why was it a sad day for Preecha (p.38)? Was he right to be sad?	People began stealing from the shops when the power went down (p.18). Why? How do you feel about that?	Uga was told not to follow Tig, but he did. Do you think he was right to follow? Explain why.	Why do you think Ahmed told the old man he didn't know Bozan and the other boys (p.15)?	Tamerlane decides to help the boy. Why? Did you think he would?
Relating to different contexts	What is your favourite film? Why do you like it?	Have you ever had something that was hard to look after? What did you do?	How would you be affected if there was a major power cut in your home or at school?	Tig really wants to be an artist. Do you know what you would like to be when you grow up?	On p.19, Ahmed decided not to tell his friends about Bozan crying. Do you think he was right not to?	Does the story of Tamerlane and the Boy remind you of any other stories you have read?

Reading Assessment

Pathfinders Strand 1

Comprehension Assessment

Book Title _____

Name: _____

Class Group: _____

Date: _____

Summarising task:

Reading task

Pages read _____

Reading Accuracy

Reading Fluency

Questions to assess understanding

Recalling:

Understanding vocabulary:

Inferring:

Responding:

Relating to different contexts:

Summary of Reading comprehension skills

Recommendations

Move to Strand 2? Y/N

Reading Assessment

Wayfarers Strand 2

Comprehension Assessment

Book Title _____

Name: _____

Class Group: _____

Date: _____

Summarising task:

Reading task

Pages read _____

Reading Accuracy

Reading Fluency

Questions to assess understanding

Recalling:

Understanding vocabulary:

Inferring:

Responding:

Relating to different contexts:

Summary of Reading comprehension skills

Recommendations

Move to Strand 3? Y/N

Reading Assessment

Explorers Strand 3

Comprehension Assessment

Book Title _____

Name: _____

Class Group: _____

Date: _____

Summarising task:

Reading task

Pages read _____

Reading Accuracy

Reading Fluency

Questions to assess understanding

Recalling:

Understanding vocabulary:

Inferring:

Responding:

Relating to different contexts:

Summary of Reading comprehension skills

Recommendations

Move to Strand 4? Y/N

Reading Assessment

Voyagers Strand 4

Comprehension Assessment

Book Title _____

Name: _____

Class Group: _____

Date: _____

Summarising task:

Reading task

Pages read _____

Reading Accuracy

Reading Fluency

Questions to assess understanding

Recalling:

Understanding vocabulary:

Inferring:

Responding:

Relating to different contexts:

Summary of Reading comprehension skills

Recommendations

Pathfinders Strand 1
Comprehension Assessment

Name: Abida
Class Group: Tigers
Date: 07.12.17

Title River Rescue

Summarising task:

Abida retold the story confidently and in the correct sequence. She referred to the text to clarify a few details, such as which of the two boys went first across the river. She added personal commentary, stating that she thought the two boys were silly to go on the river when the weather forecast was bad, and that their dad should have looked after them.

Reading task
Pages read 10 to 18

Reading Accuracy
Reading generally accurate. Some inflectional 'ed' endings missed but likely to be linked to her pronunciation of these words in English. Some sounding out along words which are unfamiliar to her ('stranded', 'dangled'). On p.16, she missed out the word 'light' then reread the whole sentence to correct this omission. She asked for my help on the words 'skywards' and 'surface'.

Reading Fluency
Abida attended to the text for clues in how to use expression as she read character voices (for example, when Mr Pattama yelled out on p.16). She noted speech punctuation, using this to change her voice when reading as a character. Some more stilted reading of longer narrative sections, and some confusion when reading more complex sentences, such as on p.18.

Questions to assess understanding

Recalling:

Abida said 'they would not have time to get here and the boys might die in the river'.

Understanding vocabulary:

She used the text to help her, and told me, 'it's when the river goes very fast and comes over the sides'. She did not refer to the landslip which contributed to the speed of the flood.

Inferring:

First answered literally ('it would fall in the river'). When prompted was able to give a more inferential answer ('maybe the rope would be near so one of the boys could grab it').

Responding:

Abida thought Kamon was brave: 'he likes doing brave things, and he had a good idea to save the boys'. She was very concerned that the boys should not have been on the river: 'their dad should have not let them'.

Relating to different contexts

Abida was able to answer as the character: 'I think I would be very pleased that I saved the two little boys, but cross with their dad for letting them take their boats in the river'. I asked 'do you think Kamon will go kayaking again?' 'I think he might be scared next time, and he will like to fly his aeroplane (drone) instead'.

Summary of Reading comprehension skills

Abida was able to summarise the story in a short retelling, adding personal detail and opinion. She read mostly accurately. She appealed when words were unknown, but noticed errors of omission, rereading to self-correct. She read speech passages accurately, although found reading longer more complex passages more difficult.

In the comprehension tasks, Abida was able to recall information directly in the text, although needed some prompting to infer what might have happened in the story if the drone had crashed. Her answers were also influenced by her concern for the small boys and why they were out on the river on their own. She didn't note information in the text to aid her definition of a flash flood, but gave a reasonable description.

Recommendations

Abida initially struggled with books in the Pathfinders strand, and previous assessments suggested she remain at that strand. It is pleasing to see the progress she has made over this term, and she is ready to move on. Attention will be needed to maintain fluency especially on longer, more complex sentences, as this may affect her comprehension. Also, to watch for appeals to the teacher, prompting her 'what can you do to solve that word?' or 'what do you know that can help you?' when she stops at unknown words.

Move to Strand 2?

Yes

Name: Vijay
Class Group: Group 3
Date: 06.10.17

Title The Changing Climate

Summarising task:

Vijay told me the book was about how skyscrapers are built and whether people like to live in them. He made no reference to the book being part historical (i.e. about how skyscrapers were developed).

Reading task

Pages read 2 to 7

Reading Accuracy

When coming to a word he did not know, Vijay tended to solve at word level (sounding out) which at times proved unsuccessful. He neglected to use syllable chunks for some longer words (such as 'manufacturing'). He lost his place occasionally on pages with denser passages (such as page 4), and needed to reread to gather meaning.

Reading Fluency

On occasions, Vijay's reading was a little too fast. He tended to neglect some of the punctuation in longer complex sentences, which affected his comprehension.

Questions to assess understanding

Recalling:

Vijay used the book to locate the information to support his retell, and was able to find the name of the inventor. He also added additional information - 'It was Mr Elisha Otis. He came from America, and he showed people how it worked.'

Understanding vocabulary:

Vijay was not able to answer the question from the assessment grid, and did not seem confident to have a go, even when directed to look at the picture of the Flatiron Building.

Inferring:

Vijay gave two reasons why there were no skyscrapers before 1880, referring back to the text: 'people didn't know how to build lifts to get people to the top of a skyscraper, and people could not make iron to make a building strong'. This indicated a clear understanding of this part of the text.

Responding:

Vijay felt there are too many skyscrapers today, and gave a very full answer: 'People have to have a garden to play in and to grow vegetables, and they need to see trees, and it is hard to get up in the building because if the lifts break you can't get up the stairs, and if you're old that is hard.'

Relating to different contexts

When asked to think of a good reason to live in a skyscraper, Vijay thought for a while and turned back to the book, looking at the picture of the Burj Khalifa on p.26 for inspiration: 'I think it would be good to be up in the sky and see the aeroplanes and the birds, and you can't see them all that well from down on the ground'.

Summary of Reading comprehension skills

Vijay was able to give a short summary of the text, picking up on some but not all of the aspects. He had some difficulty when attempting to read words he had not seen before, in particular seeming to neglect chunking word into syllable parts. He read fast, often un-phrased and missing commas, which affected the depth of his comprehension.

Vijay seemed to really enjoy the book and was keen to talk about it. He was able to respond to most questions appropriately, but was hesitant to attempt a response if unsure.

Recommendations

Concerns about fluent reading and limited attention to punctuation, along with unhelpful problem solving at points of difficulty lead to a decision to remain reading at this strand for a while longer. A focus on fiction stories will help encourage fluent reading and teaching will focus on independent strategies to problem-solve and prompting to self-monitor the sound of reading and to attend to punctuation.

Move to Strand 2?

No - accuracy and comprehension are not evidenced as fluent - not a good basis for the next strand.